MISSOURI

RIVER

RIVER

MISSISSIPPI

KANSAS
LANDING

INDEPENDENCE

ST. LOUIS

ARKANSAS   RIVER

CAIRO

OHIO   RIVER

RIVER

PITTSBURGH

CROSSROADS OF AMERICA

THE STORY OF KANSAS CITY

DARRELL GARWOOD

CROSSROADS OF AMERICA

THE STORY OF KANSAS CITY

W · W · NORTON & COMPANY · INC · *New York*

977.8411
G19c

24841
Dec 48

Book Design by John Woodlock

TO
HELEN

Contents

Illustrations

Foreword

THE STORY OF KANSAS CITY to a large extent has been a history of the country, in miniature, for the last one hundred years. In the beginning, steamboats and wagon caravans came here from far parts of the continent. The city was an important battleground during the Civil War. Afterward influences from East, West, North and South converged and joined in the building of the city. Today Kansas City stands poised on the edge of the Great Plains states, a transportation hub through which seven million railroad passengers travel each year.

Different influences in the city's development were represented in strong personalities, some of whom are included in this book. I have attempted in each period to associate the best-known personalities with the main facts concerning the city, and then to connect the whole in a narrative as nearly continuous as the subject would permit.

Before doing the research on this subject, I interviewed, or just talked to, a large number of people in the city and its vicinity. Sometimes I went to offices or homes, and sometimes I started conversations with people who were sitting in the parks. In both cases, I found informants who could tell a great deal of the region's past, and who were proud of the fact that the city had played a key role in stirring and dramatic events.

My deepest appreciation goes to all the people with whom I talked. I am especially indebted to the following: Mr. and Mrs. Thornton Cooke, who in my behalf invited to their home many persons whom otherwise I would not have met; Mr. and Mrs. Louis Shouse, who both gave me their recollections and did research for me; Mr. James Anderson and Mr. George Fuller Green, of the Kansas City Native Sons' Society, who gave me the advantage of their wide reading and the use of the collected material in the library maintained by their society; the Kansas City *Star* and many members of the *Star's* editorial staff, especially James S. Jackson and Charles Blood, and the members of the *Star's* library staff, who over a period of months obtained information from the files for me on all the subjects in which I was interested.

I am also indebted to the Library of Congress, especially to the people in its local history, manuscript and newspaper reference divisions. The published and written sources of information are acknowledged at the end of the book.

Darrell Garwood

CHAPTER ONE

Gateway to India

THE YEAR WAS 1845. Senator Thomas Hart Benton, Missouri's leading historical figure, was approaching the town of Kansas aboard one of the twin-funneled, wood-burning steamboats that plied the Missouri. At that time a large portion of the continent west of Missouri was designated on maps simply as the "Great American Desert." Trade with the Mexican city of Santa Fé had been in progress for twenty-five years, but the great migration across the Rocky Mountains and to the west coast was just getting under way. The town of Kansas, which was to become Kansas City, consisted of a few houses and two or three warehouses, crowded by bluffs onto the Missouri River's edge.

Senator Benton was a man of large and splendid physique, wearing his usual stiff top hat, satin vest, long blue cloak, pantaloons and low shoes with white stockings. His piercing eyes were set under a high, domelike forehead, and his large bony nose bent down over a small mouth. With a group of other men, he stood at the deck rail looking out over the river. As the boat pushed upward against the current, he lifted one arm toward the scraggly line of river bluffs on which Kansas City later located, and said:

"Gentlemen, there is the gateway to India."

The remark was a characteristic one for Benton, and his meaning was well understood by men of the day. Years before, Benton had pointed out that the rivers and trails of America offered a possible route to Asia, "direct, safe, cheap and exclusively American," and twenty thousand miles shorter than the route of the clipper ships. The westward movement was sure to lead to a prosperous oriental trade. And Benton believed that the town of Kansas would become the important junction between the river steamboats and the wagon trails used in the transcontinental migration.

Steamboats from Pittsburgh, Pennsylvania, could cruise nine hundred and fifty miles down the Ohio River to the Mississippi. They could then switch up the Mississippi to St. Louis, and from there could proceed another two hundred and fifty miles westward by steaming up the Missouri to the point of Kansas City. However, because the course up the Missouri turned northward here, there was no navigable river to carry the steamboats westward beyond the town of Kansas. This geographical location made the town's site an ideal base to serve as a western terminal for the steamboats.

But because of its bluffs, Kansas offered a poor site for a town. Near-by Independence, Missouri, long head of the older Santa Fé Trail, was serving also as the head of the newly opened California and Oregon trails. The steamboat landing for Independence was fourteen miles downstream from Kansas. It was Benton's prediction that, despite handicaps of terrain, the principal landing on the river would move upstream to the town of Kansas, which would then become the head of the wagon trails into the Far West.

Senator Benton had a long public career, covering the period when the tide of westward migration was moving up from the Old South, across Tennessee and Kentucky, and across the Mississippi River, into Missouri. He was born in North Carolina and before going West had attended the University of North Carolina. At the age of twenty-one, he was already on the frontier in Tennessee when the territory of Missouri and other lands beyond the Mississippi were acquired by the Louisiana Purchase of 1803. He was elected to the Tennessee State Senate, rose to the rank of Colonel in the Tennessee militia, and for several years served as aide-de-camp to Major General Andrew Jackson.

His stay in Tennessee was cut short by a celebrated quarrel with Jackson. General Jackson acted as second for a man who fought a duel with one of Benton's brothers. Infuriated by this action, Benton accused Jackson of conducting the duel in an unfair manner. Jackson retorted that he would horsewhip Tom Benton the first time he saw him; and, when the two men met in Nashville, he attempted to carry out his threat. As Jackson advanced on Benton, he was shot down by Benton's brother. There ensued a general free-for-all between the partisans of the antagonists, in the course of which Benton twice fired a pistol without effect, and in backing away from an assailant fell down a flight of steps.

Jackson was seriously wounded, while the Bentons were largely unhurt. They claimed the victory, and proceeded to break Jackson's sword in the public square as evidence of their disdain for him. They also sent all their friends a notice giving their side of the argument. However, Jackson's stature was growing: he was soon to become the most popular and powerful man in Tennessee. His friends harried Benton because of the old quarrel so effectively that Benton moved on to the Territory of Missouri, settling in 1815 at St. Louis, at that time a town of some two thousand people. He published a small St. Louis newspaper and was active in public affairs.

Christopher (Kit) Carson, whose fame was to become linked to Benton's, preceded him on the Missouri scene by four years. Carson had come as a year-old infant with one of several Kentucky parties, consisting in all of some one hundred and fifty families, who arrived at intervals during 1810 and 1811. These families greatly advanced the settlement of the territory by moving two hundred miles west along the Missouri River to occupy some attractive bottom lands that were suitable for the growing of tobacco. On this new frontier in central Missouri, they founded the town of Franklin and built five forts, each fort consisting of twenty or thirty cabins placed around a square, animals and tools being kept in the enclosure thus formed. Kit Carson's earliest recollections were of life in one of these forts,—of men working in the fields while other men stood guard with rifles at the borders of the cultivated land. Despite these precautions, ten settlers were killed by Indians in the first seven years of the settlement.

By 1817, the Indians of the vicinity were peaceful, and political organization had caught up with the frontier. The settlement's town of Franklin on the Missouri was made a county seat. In 1819 for the first time, two steamboats ascended the Missouri, and were greeted at Franklin with much feasting and celebration. Toasts were drunk to the Missouri River, to Robert Fulton, to Benjamin Franklin, to the United States Government, and to various governmental officials. Four years later, in 1821, Missouri was admitted to the Union

GATEWAY TO INDIA 17

as a slaveholding state. In that same year Mexico gained its independence from Spain and opened its doors to trade.

By this time Carson, a boy of twelve, had heard much talk of the possibilities of trade with the Mexican city of Santa Fé, eight hundred miles to the southwest. Fifteen men left Franklin in 1821 with pack mules laden with goods to sell in Santa Fé, and they brought back reports of good prices received—as much as two dollars a yard for calico cloth. Santa Fé possessed considerable silver; it was deep inland, remote from all factories and transportation. Franklin, Missouri, was closer to it than any seaport town. In 1822 three wagons were used to haul goods to Santa Fé, and soon caravans of twenty to forty wagons were moving over the Santa Fé Trail. In the same years, 1822 and 1823, the first of the American fur-trapping expeditions passed up the Missouri River. In their company were Jim Bridger, Thomas Fitzpatrick, Captain Bill Sublette, all famous mountain men in later times. Streams in the unexplored half of the continent were full of beaver, and during the early years beaver pelts were in good demand for making hats. The steamboats brought goods up the river and took furs back.

Carson's father having been killed by a falling tree, the boy was apprenticed at an early age to a saddler in the village of Franklin. He worked two years with leather at a bench, but being "anxious to travel for the purpose of seeing different countries," he ran away at the age of sixteen, and in 1826 joined a Santa Fé caravan. He left Franklin as a "cavvy boy"; he rode a mule at a slow walk and herded the extra horses and mules through the dust raised by twenty-five or thirty canvas-topped wagons, each of which was drawn by eight mules. For the next sixteen years he trapped beaver, on both sides of the Rocky Mountains, in the Northwest and the Southwest, without returning to the Missouri Valley.

Benton, chosen as one of Missouri's first two United States Senators, was active in promoting the Santa Fé trade, and was keenly interested in anything he could learn about the Great West. He invited to his home in Washington Lieutenant John C. Frémont, of the United States Army Topographical Engineers, who had done some exploring, mapping, and charting in the nearer trans-Mississippi lands. Frémont came often to the Benton home thereafter to describe his experiences, and so met and fell in love with Benton's sixteen-year-old daughter Jessie. Moreover, she fell in love with him. Senator Benton was indignant and wrathful. Through his influence, he had Frémont sent on a minor exploring trip along the lower Des Moines River, in the hope that the romance would be forgotten. But when that expedition was completed, Frémont and Jessie were secretly married. Once the event had occurred, Benton reconciled himself to the marriage and began sponsoring his son-in-law in further and more dramatic explorations.

In 1842, the Oregon boundary dispute with the British was brewing. Though only a few hundred Americans had crossed the Rocky Mountains, Benton wished to see "forty thousand American rifles" in Oregon, for use if the British pressed their claims too far. Frémont was sent to survey the lands between Missouri and the South Pass in Wyoming, that pass serving as the principal route through the mountains for migrations to California and Oregon. He left Washington in the spring of 1842. At about the same time, from the other end of the continent, Kit Carson was joining a Santa Fé caravan for his first return to Missouri. Both Frémont and Carson were bound for the future site of Kansas City—Frémont to start his expedition and Carson to board a steamboat and to revisit his home territory.

When Carson had gone west in 1826, there was no town on

the site of Kansas City. When he returned in 1842 there were
three towns, Independence, Westport, and Kansas, which
would eventually grow together to constitute the city. The
Santa Fé wagon caravans which at first had assembled and
pushed off from Franklin, or from Arrow Rock just across the
river, had progressively moved the trailhead farther up the
river, to Independence. Westport, a few miles to the west
through which the trail passed, was a lodging town, used by
the traders because they could pasture their animals nearby.
Kansas, with a few dozen inhabitants, served as a landing for
Westport. It included a fur collection post which had been
established there in 1821 by François Chouteau, one of a large
family of fur traders from St. Louis. About thirty French-
speaking and canoe-traveling fur traders, some of them sup-
porting Indian wives, had built cabins in the bottom lands
around this post.

Independence, with two or three thousand people, was
generally regarded at the time as the place of "first and last
chance"—to sleep in a bed, to get a drink over a bar, to send a
letter home, to get a wagon repaired or to buy a yoke of oxen
or a team of mules. On the other hand, Kansas was nearer the
Southwest; and the traveler coming in on the Santa Fé Trail,
if he had no need for the services or "luxuries" of Independence, could save fourteen miles of overland travel by boarding
a steamboat there. Kit Carson had no reason for going to
Independence, so he went to Kansas, following a road which
led four miles down a ravine from Westport to the Kansas
levee. He had with him his five-year-old daughter by an
Arapaho Indian wife, described by Carson as a "good girl,"
who had died sometime after the birth of the child. He took
a boat for St. Louis, where he placed the child in a convent
school. He remained in the city a few days, but was soon
"tired of settlements," and boarded a steamboat to return to

the Kansas levee. On the same boat was Frémont, bound up
the river with twenty-three men and eight mule carts to
start his expedition. Frémont and Carson met on the boat and
fell into conversation.

Lieutenant Frémont, slender, handsome, quick and ener-
getic, spoke rapidly; Carson, long-haired, short and thickset,
long-bodied and bandy-legged from riding, replied with
measured deliberation. Frémont, twenty-nine years old, not
much younger than Carson in years but much younger in experience, was full of enthusiasm and talk concerning his forthcoming survey of the region between Missouri and the South
Pass, lands then known as the "Platte Country." Carson had
already visited California, had been through the South
Pass, and over all the ground of which Frémont was speaking.
He remarked mildly that he knew something of the "Platte
Country," and thought he could take Frémont anywhere he
might wish to go.

When Carson spoke, people usually listened. He was direct
in his speech and used the fewest possible words—the Indians
said he spoke with a single tongue. On this occasion, Frémont
immediately became interested, and said he would make in-
quiries among others on the boat regarding Carson's ability.
"I presume he received reports favorable to me," related
Carson. For he soon returned and offered Carson one hundred
dollars a month to act as his guide. In the good years the
beaver had provided the trappers with larger incomes, but
at this time silk was replacing beaver in the manufacture of
hats, and the price of beaver had gone down. Carson accepted the offer. During the next four years he was with Frémont, the Pathfinder, on the latter's three famous expeditions
into the West.

From his expeditions, Frémont sent glowing reports to
Congress, which became an important factor in stimulating

the westward migration. The same reports, lauding Carson's character and describing his exploits, made Kit Carson famous throughout the land. "With me, Carson and the truth are the same thing," said Frémont. Senator Benton always saw that Frémont's reports received extensive printing and wide distribution; and Benton himself was enabled to preside like a giant over the early movement into the West. His stature meanwhile had also increased because in Washington he had repaired his shooting quarrel with Jackson, and when Jackson was President had been one of his staunchest supporters. Besides serving for many years as the West's principal champion in the Senate, Benton in later life was often referred to as the leading Jacksonian of his time.

Frémont and Carson, in starting their expeditions, used the Kansas landing in preference to the one for Independence. This helps to explain why Benton, when Independence was still flourishing, was convinced that Kansas would be the more important town. Characteristically, Benton then carried the thought much further. In 1853, eight years after his first expression, and when the town of Kansas still had a population of less than three hundred, he made a second and even more generous prediction. On this occasion he had disembarked from a steamboat to address a group of settlers. Standing on a large rock a little below the town, he again raised an arm toward the bluffs, and said:

There, gentlemen, where the rocky bluff meets and turns aside the sweeping current of this mighty river; here, where the Missouri, after pursuing its southward course for two thousand miles, turns eastward to meet the Mississippi, a large commercial and manufacturing center will congregate, and another generation will see a great city on these hills.

Benton's stature was fully appreciated in Missouri, and, even though his political mannerisms were pompous, arrogant, and overbearing, he was generally popular with his constituents. He was given to identifying himself in the first instance as "I, Thomas H. Benton," and thereafter referring to himself in royal fashion, as "Benton." Critics often took him to task for his egotism, but Benton disdained them. "The difference between all these little men and Benton," he told one audience, "is that I *have* an Ego, and they have none."

A St. Louis newspaper once suggested that no other population on the globe would stand for such a man. However, another newspaper writer observed that Benton's airs and egotism had been carried to such a monumental height that they were beyond offense, and were regarded as a sort of national institution in which everyone ought to take pride. This was probably near the mark, since a number of admiring nicknames were applied to him—"Old Bullion," "Old Ironclad," and "The Old Mastiff."

His adherence to high principle and the general welfare could scarcely be questioned. He was immensely bold in statecraft, with a keen insight into issues. Further, he had a gift for dramatizing them. Often he employed spectacular language, as when, in defense of the Missouri Compromise, he described the Kansas-Nebraska bill as "all fraud, cheat, trick, swindle, quackery, charlatanry, demagoguery, bladdery and legislative blackleggery." When he mounted a platform in Missouri he was usually greeted by rapturous applause. After his death a statue of him was erected in Lafayette Park in St. Louis, and engraved on the base of the statue were the words he had used on several occasions in urging the westward movement: "There is the East; there is India!"

CHAPTER TWO

The Founding Fathers

INDEPENDENCE AND WESTPORT, and Chouteau's fur
collection post, were well established before the town of Kansas appeared. John C. McCoy, the principal founder of
Kansas City, was from Westport. He was early on the scene
because his father was a missionary to the Indians who held
all the land immediately to the west of Missouri. These were
peaceful Indians, members of tribes that had been moved out
of territory farther east. They received small pensions from
the government, and they came into the towns to trade, riding
across the border on shaggy ponies, for which they bought
bridles and colored ribbons.

McCoy, a square-cut man with sideburns, a surveyor and
graduate of Transylvania University in Kentucky, opened a
store in Westport for trade with the Indians. It took him a
day's hauling with an ox team to bring his goods from the
landing for Independence. Much closer, only four miles away
under the bluff, he noticed that alongside Chouteau's post

there was an excellent natural levee, a ledge of rock jutting
into the river. In 1834, he had his goods delivered to this
levee. A steamboat drew alongside, and his stock of goods
was thrown overboard to him. By chopping with an ax
through the underbrush, and felling a few trees, McCoy was
then able to haul the goods up a ravine to Westport. The
rock ledge first used by McCoy became the landing for Westport, and was the site where the town of Kansas was founded.

The founding occurred on a cold November day in 1838.
A chilling wind was blowing in off the river as a group of
twenty-five or thirty fur-capped and booted men gathered
on the levee for an auction of the late Gabrielle Prudhomme's
property. One of Prudhomme's daughters had petitioned the
Circuit Court of Jackson County for a money division of the
estate, necessitating the sale. The property abutted the Missouri River at the point of the landing, and all present recognized that it should be converted into a formal townsite.
Squire George W. Tate of Westport called for bids from a
platform which had been placed across the rails of a livestock
pen, built on the levee for the use of animals that might be
awaiting steamboat passage or ferry.

McCoy and thirteen other men had formed the "Kansas
Town Company" to bid on the property. The members of this
Town Company comprised about half the men who were
gathered on the levee for the auction. One of the members
was Captain Bill Sublette, the famous mountain man, who
had been accounted one of the best captains of trappers in
the country during the good years of the beaver. In 1838
beaver trapping had already declined, and Sublette was serving as guide for parties wishing to enter uncharted regions
of the West. Captain Sublette stood six feet two inches and
was called "Cut Face" by the Indians because of a long scar
on the left side of his chin. He was a big, good-natured fellow,

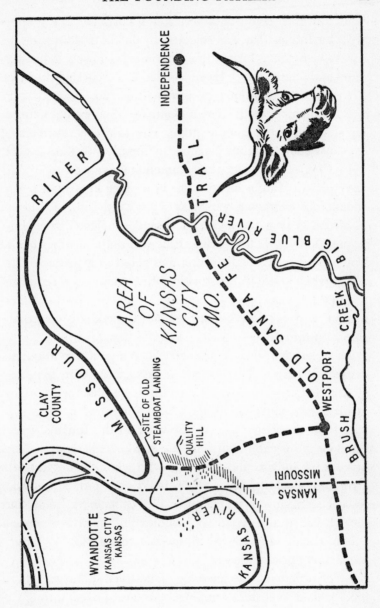

who, however, could be a very rough customer in a grapple with an Indian. He was selected to do the bidding for the Town Company. From time to time he raised a hamlike hand and offered a bid. He succeeded in purchasing the farm, 271 rugged acres of land, at a price of $4,220.

Each member of the Town Company then gave a note for his share of the purchase price. The fourteen members of McCoy's company thus became the founders of Kansas City.

In view of the cold, they immediately retired to discuss their plans before a hickory fire in a place kept by a lanky, cadaverous character known as "One-Eyed Ellis." Gathered in his cabin near the levee, the founders selected their host to preside over their meeting. Ellis was not a member of the Town Company, but he sometimes acted as a Justice of the Peace when a sale of livestock or other transaction requiring a signature was completed on the levee, and this faint connection with legal procedure seemed to make his chairmanship appropriate.

The chairmanship of the first meeting of the founders caused One-Eyed Ellis to become associated with the story of Kansas City. Otherwise he would have remained obscure in his cabin under the bluff, where he gained his living in part from the illegal sale of firewater to the Indians. From the door of his cabin, with his one good eye, he kept a sharp lookout for Indians and squatters with whom he might trade a tin cup of whisky for a coonskin—a very profitable trade, since a coonskin was worth about fifty cents in St. Louis, and the whisky he dispensed was wholesaling at fifteen cents a gallon. He also augmented his income occasionally by catching a stray horse or steer.

As chairman of the meeting, One-Eyed Ellis got out a blue-backed Webster's spelling book and leafed through it in the hope of coming upon a word that would make a good name for the new town. He apparently found nothing that appealed to the founders in the general discussion which followed. Certain of the founders later recalled that Abraham Fonda, one of their number, who wore a tail coat and liked to record his occupation as "gentleman," was insistent that the town should be called "Port Fonda"; and that someone else said he would prefer "Rabbitville" or "Possum Trot." But finally, after a good deal of bantering, they chose the name "Kansas," an Indian word which meant "smoky wind" and was used to designate prairie fires. It was also the name of an Indian tribe native to the vicinity.

The selection of the name was the most important business completed at the meeting. The following spring, in 1839, McCoy as the surveyor of the group laid off a small part of the land. Soon afterward ten lots in the town of Kansas were sold. McCoy's partial plat, showing the ten lots, was filed at the courthouse in Independence. And for a number of years his plat was the only official indication that such a town existed. The next official record was made in 1846, and was to the effect that the Prudhomme heirs were suing the founders, individually and collectively, for payment of their notes.

Had it not been that McCoy was a "writing man," the record would merely show that in 1846 court judgments were taken against each of the founders on his note, and that in seven years not one of them had made a single dollar of payment to the Prudhomme heirs. McCoy himself was a little apologetic about this feature of the founding. However, he explained that what actually occurred might be described as a test case, caused by a number of technical legal questions which had arisen.

After the first two or three meetings it had proved to be impossible ever to get the founders together again—a situation which is understandable. Captain Bill Sublette, for instance, would be off guiding parties over the plains or through the mountains, and several others followed nomadic occupations. It had even been impossible to get proper signatures on some of the legal documents related to the townsite. Presently it was suggested that perhaps the Kansas Town Company did not have a clear title to the land.

As a result, after a number of delays, McCoy and others who were on the ground decided to let the Prudhommes sue for their money, so that a court could decide the legal questions involved, and thus establish a clear title to the land. Certain founders took over the interests of others who were either absent or embarrassed for funds, until the number of founders had been pared to five. These five pooled their resources in a fund to pay the Prudhommes when a court order should be entered. Once the judgments were taken, in 1846, the Prudhommes promptly received their money.

This proved to be an opportune settlement of the Town Company's affairs. Eighteen hundred and forty-six was the year of the Mexican War, and considerable quantities of military supplies were being routed through to the Southwest. Between forty and fifty steamboats operated on the Missouri to bring up men and guns. The factor which formerly had held back the town of Kansas, its bluffs and generally poor townsite, did not enter into the calculations of the military men. Their chief consideration was the fact that the Kansas levee was the landing closest to their destination. Another consideration was that the Kansas River emptied into the Missouri not far above the loading point while the Big Blue River emptied into the Missouri below it. These two rivers, the Kansas and the Big Blue, opened out in such a way that by starting from the Kansas levee it was possible to reach the Southwest without fording either of them—an important advantage when the streams were swollen. Further, the excellent natural levee, the ledge of rock, made this one of the few places where the churning Missouri River could not shift in its bed.

From 1831 until the Mexican War, Independence had held its position as the head of the trails. It had enjoyed a fifteen-year monopoly of the wagon-outfitting business. It had dispatched as many as four hundred a year of the big Pittsburgh wagons used in the Santa Fé trade, each wagon being drawn by twelve steers or oxen. But when the military supplies began going through the town of Kansas, the traders and emigrants tended to follow—the "short cut" was becoming the main route. Independence lost its grip on the trails just as the big surge toward the West was about to begin. After the Mexican War came the California gold rush of 1848–49 when forty thousand men passed through this territory, spending five million dollars for wagons, animals, and supplies. And not long after the gold rush, more than ten thousand wagons of all descriptions left each year, carrying the settlers who preceded the railroads into the West, over the trails that had been marked out by Frémont and Carson.

As late as 1849, Independence still had some hope of holding a large share of the traffic. During that year the town built a mule-powered railroad which ran the six miles to its landing —the first railroad west of the Mississippi. But whatever chance the railroad had of diverting the flow of traffic back to Independence was obliterated in one night when the Missouri shifted in its bed and threw up a sand bar which ruined the landing. By 1850, five years after Senator Benton had predicted its new role, the town of Kansas had become well established as the principal landing on the river.

But the principal landing was not yet the principal town. At first the wagon-outfitting business shifted to Westport. Then for several years the residents of the vicinity seemed unwilling to recognize the landing's identity as a town. People living in Westport referred to it simply as "the landing," while in Independence it was called "Westport Landing." It was also called "Chouteau's Warehouse" and "Kawsmouth," the Kansas River being known locally as the Kaw. The name "Westport Landing" was even used on maps and in postal guides. But the correct name from the beginning, by the founders' decision, was "Kansas," and this was the name used by Benton, Frémont, and Carson.

In the middle 1850's some of the wagon freighters, ignoring Westport, began loading from steamboats on the Kansas levee, and gradually the wagon-outfitting business shifted to the town of Kansas. At about the same time, the Kansas Territory lying immediately to the west was opened for settlement, and settlers began arriving in great numbers to occupy those lands. These developments, together with the increasing migration to the Far West, made it apparent to everyone that a city of some size would one day rise on this spot.

None of the original founders profited largely from the city's growth. Each had disposed of his holdings at a time seemingly opportune, but before the big development occurred. McCoy often said in his later years that they had no idea they were founding a city, their principal purpose in forming the Town Company having been to "make a few dollars." However, as the city grew, François Chouteau made a small fortune from the land he had acquired with his fur-collection post. Surviving Chouteaus operated a steamboat on the Missouri, and one of them held several offices in city administrations.

For One-Eyed Ellis the developments brought a gain in public notice. As early as 1855 the word "City" was commonly added to the word "Kansas" as the name of the place. The fact that One-Eyed Ellis seventeen years earlier had served as chairman of the founders' meeting was frequently recalled. One of the founders remarked concerning the Ellis chairmanship: "It was his only claim to celebrity, too, except that he sold remarkably bad whisky to the Indians."

The "city" before the Civil War closely resembled an overgrown western town of later times. Its main street was lined with flat frame buildings, a row of saloons, board sidewalks and hitching rails. Wholesale merchants operated in two- and three-story buildings with porches, and large butcher shops served as packing houses, where pork was put into barrels for shipment abroad. The city's population was variously estimated at four thousand to seventy-five hundred, depending on how much of the shifting population of migrants was counted. At either the high or the low figure, it was big enough to be called a "city," in a day when the average town consisted of a few houses and a crossroads store.

In order to create an uptown section which could be reached from the rock levee, streets were dug through the north bluffs. Several cuts of thirty and forty feet were required, and the canyons created by the digging of streets were the subject of first comments concerning the city. There were suggestions that along these streets the houses might be more conveniently built from top to bottom. An early newspaper description of Kansas City ran: "Its houses stand some of them with the roof toward the street and some with the foundation. Its streets cross each other perpendicularly or something like it, at angles as regular as zig-zag lightning chasing amatory tomcats. City property is divided into three sorts, to wit: improved property, vacant lots and sites for lots." Nevertheless the streets served their purpose. By the time of the Civil War the uptown section, above the bluff, had acquired one good three-story brick hotel, the Pacific House, and several lesser hotels; two daily newspapers, a theater called an Opera House, and a residential section stretching toward Westport.

The principal center of business was still the levee, where on clear days several hundred wagons would leave for the West. Steamboat dockings increased to seven hundred a year, and merchandise was piled up for several blocks along the river. Crowds gathered on the levee, and bullwhackers went among them to clear a path for the wagons. This was the main junction for continent-wide traffic by water and wagon. The buckskin of mountaineers mingled with the blue jeans of stevedores and squatters, and the tail coats and top hats of "gentlemen"—a gentleman being any property owner. Or the same formal attire might indicate a steamboat gambler. Women of the day wore sunbonnets. Some owners of real-estate subdivisions met all the steamboats with brass bands and banners advertising their lots, and the steamboats brought bands for dances that were commonly held on their decks. This period became known as the "era of boats," a relatively short era lasting only six years.

While travel to the Far West steadily increased, the most immediate contribution to the city's pre-Civil War activity was the opening of the adjacent Kansas Territory. For many years the flat buffalo plains which could be seen sweeping westward from Kansas City's bluffs had been regarded as part of the "Great American Desert"; but when the better lands of the region had been taken up, the plains began to seem desirable. Lieutenant Frémont had been more optimistic than earlier explorers concerning living conditions on the "desert," and Senator Benton had been encouraged to say that the country "ought to be habitable along its rivers and

streams." By the time of the actual opening of the Kansas
Territory in 1854, there must have been in the country an
excellent opinion of its value, judging by the speed with which
settlers arrived with their agricultural implements.

These settlers came up the Missouri River in steamboats.
Some of them went forty miles farther up the river to Leavenworth, and settled in the northern part of the territory; but
more of them landed at Kansas City. From the beginning,
although located across the border in Missouri, Kansas City
served as the principal city and distribution center for the
state of Kansas. In 1857 the river front Gilliss House registered
twenty-seven thousand arrivals, nearly all of them settlers
bound for Kansas.

The settlement of Kansas was occurring more than forty
years after Kit Carson's party migrated into central Missouri,
more than thirty years after Missouri was admitted to state-
hood, and more than twenty years after Missouri was fully
settled to its western border. During these time lapses, the
North had steadily industrialized, had greatly increased its
population, and had endangered the pre-eminent position
which the South had always held in the councils of the nation.
There were border troubles between Missouri and Kansas
almost from the opening of the territory, but they at first did
not interfere with the growth of the city. With the outbreak
of the Civil War in 1861, however, the growth stopped
altogether and the city temporarily declined.

CHAPTER THREE

Border War

MUCH OF THE BLOODY HISTORY of Kansas City and its immediate vicinity resulted from the fact that the city stood at a border point where the settlement of the West by Southerners ended, and where settlement by Northerners began. Southern influence stopped at Missouri's western edge when Northern settlers moved in great numbers into the Kansas Territory. After a struggle, the Northerners gained the upper hand politically in Kansas. Many Southerners who had intended to settle in the territory were driven back into Missouri, and the Kansas-Missouri border became the dividing line between different peoples.

The Missouri Compromise of 1820 had decreed that all western territory lying this far north should be forever free. Over Benton's strenuous protests, the Missouri Compromise was repealed in 1854, in favor of the Kansas-Nebraska bill, with its doctrine of "Squatter's Sovereignty," of self-determination in the matter of slavery. Since Missouri, a slaveholding state, formed the territory's entire eastern border, it seemed probable that Kansas would become a Slave State. For this reason many antislavery men from the North hurried to the scene to help prevent such development. Among the first arrivals were the five stalwart sons of Old John Brown—Old Brown himself was to join them a little later.

En route to Kansas City two of the Browns—John Brown, Jr., and his brother Jason—chanced, at St. Louis, to board a steamboat whose passengers were mostly Southerners. In the luggage which the Browns dragged aboard was a box of young fruit trees and grapevines which they had planned to set out when they reached Kansas; they had also brought with them a steel plow and various other agricultural implements. John Brown, Jr., noted in a letter to his father that the Southerners did not appear to have any agricultural equipment, and many of them wore large revolvers and Bowie knives stuck prominently in their belts. He further noted that most of the Southerners, including the boat crew, were extremely hostile to him and to the few other Northerners aboard.

This hostility became more evident when the Browns went ashore at Waverly, Missouri, to bury Jason's son, who had died of cholera. Without warning, the captain of the steamboat cast off and left them there, although they had paid their fare to Kansas City. The Browns then made a journey of two days overland. They were unable to buy food until they arrived at Kansas City: at each farmhouse where they stopped they were told, "We have nothing for you." After the Browns had settled with their families near the newly established town of Ossawatomie, Kansas, forty-five miles southwest of Kansas City, they learned much more of the anti-Yankee and proslavery sentiment which was being organized against them in Missouri.

The slavery issue, during the maneuvers that preceded the opening of the Kansas Territory, had tended to realign Missouri sectionally, and to place it with the Southern instead of the Western states. Benton, although Southern in origin, had always been thought of as a Western senator. But he was national in his point of view, he understood the danger of civil war, and he saw the change with alarm. "How, but with the aid of Northern votes," he asked, "are we to get the transcontinental railroad which is the prayer of every good man in Missouri?" Moreover, although himself an owner of slaves, Benton stood against the extension of slavery. "My profession and conduct do not agree," he admitted. "My sentiments, then, are against the institution of slavery, and against its introduction into places in which it does not exist."

Powerful and large though his following was, Benton's stand meant his political doom. Missouri had 100,000 slaves, valued at $100,000,000; its people were Southern in origin; and the South was demanding more Slave States to offset the growing Northwest and maintain the Southern margin of votes in Congress. These factors sent Benton, in 1850, down in defeat, after thirty years in office. He later served a term in the lower house of Congress, and ran unsuccessfully for governor, but he never again entered the United States Senate. At the time of the actual opening of the Kansas Territory, the most conspicuous political figure in Missouri was Benton's bitterest enemy, the proslavery Senator David R. Atchison.

Under Senator Atchison's active leadership, caravans and parties of Missourians were organized to take part in the Kansas elections. A congressional investigation later showed that in the election of March 30, 1855, when 2,905 Kansans were qualified to vote, 6,307 votes had been cast. At first these Missouri voting expeditions were carried out in a picnic spirit. At some of the Kansas polling places distant from the border,

the nonresident voters camped overnight outside the town.
The next day they entered the town to vote. If any question
of residence was raised, the Missourians presented revolvers
as evidence of their eligibility. The Free State Kansans were
unable to stop them; and the national government at Washington, poised between the sharp horns of the sectional issue,
was not disposed to interfere. After the balloting, wagon
drivers passed among the voters calling, "All aboard to Kansas
City and Westport," and other Missouri destinations. The
result of this kind of voting was the election of a completely
proslavery Kansas territorial legislature, some of whose
members were residents of Missouri.

John Brown, Jr., wrote to his father about the situation on
May 20, 1855: "While the interest of despotism has secured to
its cause hundreds and thousands of the meanest and most
desperate men, armed to the teeth with Revolvers, Bowie
Knives, Rifles and Cannon . . . the friends of freedom are
not one-fourth of them half armed, and as for military organization among them it nowhere exists in this Territory unless
they have recently done something at Lawrence. The result
of this is that the people here exhibit the most abject and
cowardly spirit whenever their dearest rights are invaded and
trampled down by the lawless bands of Miscreants which
Missouri has ready at a moment's call to pour in upon them.
. . . They boast that they can obtain possession of the polls
in any of our election precincts without having to fire a gun.
. . . In the language of a memorial recently signed by the
people here and sent to Congress petitioning help, 'It is no
longer a question of negro slavery, but the enslavement of
ourselves.' "

The younger Brown went on to say that, in order to be
properly armed, each of the five sons must have two revolvers,
a rifle and a Bowie knife. He asked his father to send them

these weapons. The elder John Brown, when he received the letter, was attending a convention of a group called the "Radical Political Abolitionists," in Syracuse, New York. He read his son's letter to the convention, took up a collection to buy weapons, and obtained sixty dollars. He later held other meetings farther west and took up more collections. When he had in hand sufficient funds and had purchased the weapons, he decided to make sure of their safe arrival by himself delivering them to his sons. Consequently, in the summer of 1855, Old John Brown set out for Kansas with a one-horse wagon so overloaded with guns, ammunition and other luggage that he and his companions were obliged to walk.

Although Brown was only fifty-five and was far from being decrepit, he was always referred to as "Old Brown," and was even described as "an aged man." He had a patriarchal air— measured tread, stooped shoulders, piercing eye and a biblical way of speaking, and the zeal of a prophet. When he reached the ferry at Brunswick, Missouri, an elderly Missourian asked him where he was from and how he was "on the goose," as the saying went. Brown replied that he was from New York, originally Ohio, and that he was Free State. "You won't live to get there," said the Missourian, with his thoughts on recent disturbances in Kansas. Whereupon Brown, glancing at his wagon, made a remark which there was afterward reason to recall. "We are prepared," he said, "not to die alone."

By the time Old Brown and his horse cart reached Kansas, in October, 1855, the Free State party was receiving supplies of Sharp's rifles, some of which were smuggled up to the river in boxes marked "books" or "Bibles." In places the Free State men had acquired sufficient strength to defy the proslavery legislature. Soon afterward they organized their own Free State legislature, and Kansas had two legislatures, each refusing to recognize the other. For the next year, a condition like guerilla war prevailed. A total of two hundred people, most of them Kansas settlers, were killed in various murders, lynchings, and skirmishes. In some cases abolitionists, or so-called abolitionists, were hunted down and shot more or less for sport, by bands of "Border Ruffians."

Much of the action centered around Lawrence, Kansas, an often-beleaguered town. Lawrence was a community of two thousand people and was the principal Free State town—located in Douglas County, Kansas, forty miles west of Kansas City.

The proslavery sheriff of Douglas County was Samuel J. Jones, who was also the postmaster at Westport, Missouri, and resided in Missouri while acting as a sheriff in Kansas. The Free State men defied his authority; he had much difficulty in making arrests; and he eventually was shot and wounded.

Sheriff Jones twice called for aid in enforcing the law. Both times small civilian armies of Missourians and pro-Southern Kansans assembled to besiege the town of Lawrence. After some parleying the first army of twelve hundred men was persuaded to leave peacefully. But the second army, on May 21, 1856, entered Lawrence, burned several houses, and de-molished the Free State Hotel with thirty-two rounds of cannon fire. Senator Atchison was present and he fired the first cannon ball into the Hotel. This event became known as the sacking of Lawrence.

John Brown and his now well-armed sons and neighbors, living thirty miles to the south of Lawrence, were summoned to the aid of the town both times it was besieged. On the first occasion they arrived in time to take part in the parleying, Old Brown making two or three fiery speeches. The second time they were on the road en route to Lawrence, when a messenger arrived to say that the town had already been de-stroyed. Thereupon they went into camp in a high state of rage and indignation. A council was held at which Old Brown favored "making an example" of some of the Southerners. Among the men present was one who had had some trouble with his proslavery neighbors at a settlement called Dutch Henry's Crossing, where Pottawatomie Creek was crossed by a road leading from Fort Scott, Kansas, to the Santa Fé Trail.

A party of eight including this man, Old Brown, and four of his sons went to Dutch Henry's Crossing. Old John Brown was the "captain" of the detachment. Near midnight on the night of May 24, 1856, they called out five pro-Southern men and killed them. Three of the victims, a father and two sons, were from Tennessee; a fourth was from Missouri and the fifth was a member of the proslavery legislature. Each was taken about one hundred yards from his home and cut down with sabers. Two of Brown's sons took part in the actual executions, and Old Brown himself, as commander of the detachment, was fully responsible. Thus for the first time John Brown became a symbolic figure in the issue which was to tear the country apart. The North was outraged by the sacking of Lawrence, and the South was equally bitter about the murders on Pottawatomie Creek.

During the succeeding summer of 1856, Missouri took effective, if unofficial, action to close the Missouri River to Northern settlers. Senator Atchison was again active, heading a party which refused to let Northern settlers disembark at Kansas City, forcing them to return to Illinois. Other parties of Missourians boarded steamboats at points along the river: they confiscated the arms of Northerners and forced them to turn back. Meanwhile Senator Atchison and other Missouri leaders prepared to menace Kansas with an even bigger civilian army. This time they raised twenty-seven hundred men, uniformed and divided into infantry and cavalry, with a strong artillery battery.

In spite of all Missouri could do, more Northerners than Southerners continued to reach Kansas. And the national administration of President Pierce, although moderately pro-Southern, could not indefinitely sanction the government of a territory by others than the people who were living in it. So Federal troops were finally ordered into action. When in September of 1856 Senator Atchison advanced upon Lawrence with the third Missouri army to threaten that town, he was intercepted by these United States troops. The Missourians were persuaded to return home. This was Missouri's last attempt to save Kansas for the South.

Thereafter there was no real doubt of the outcome. The Missouri River again was thrown open to Northern settlers. Fifty thousand of them arrived in the spring of 1857, and the Free State men that year captured the Kansas elections by a majority of three to one. The South did not have the population to compete with the North in settlement, and in any case Kansas was unsuited to Southern agriculture. The question remaining was whether Kansas could be brought into the Union as a Free State. This finally occurred on January 29, 1861, after Southern Representatives had withdrawn from Congress as a preliminary to the Civil War.

But before that, beginning in 1857, the border warfare had taken a new turn. Instead of Missourians invading Kansas, bands of armed Kansans visited themselves upon the Missouri countryside. Their avowed purpose was to free slaves, but they also took whatever other property they could conveniently bring out.

Old John Brown conducted one such raid into Missouri, in December, 1858. He and his men visited the homes of three slaveholders, shot and killed one who resisted, and came out with eleven Negroes and several wagonloads of incidental supplies. Brown took the Negroes north on the overland route through Iowa and into Canada, where under Canadian law they were free. The ease with which this had been accomplished on the turbulent Missouri border apparently encouraged Brown to undertake a much bolder project, in the quiet and distant state of Virginia. In the fall of 1859 he descended upon the sleepy village of Harper's Ferry, Virginia, with an "army" of twenty-two men. He took some prisoners and seized the United States arsenal. Upon the arrival of a few Virginia troops, the arsenal was besieged, and he was wounded and captured. While he was held in Virginia, there was talk in Kansas of raising a force to attempt his rescue, but the attempt was never carried out, and he was tried and executed under Virginia law.

James H. Lane, later United States Senator from Kansas, and James Montgomery and Charles Jennison, both of whom rose to colonelcies in the Union Army, were leaders of other raiding parties which invaded Missouri. The raiding back and forth across the border continued for ten years—six years before the Civil War and four years of the war itself. Each side sympathized with its own victims. Lane, Montgomery and Jennison, whose names were as well known as any in the history of this section, were heroes on one side of the border, villains on the other. John Brown was wholly justified in Kansas, and wholly condemned in Missouri. To both sides he became a symbol. The Kansans with the rest of the North sang "John Brown's body . . . his soul goes marching on," while the Confederates in Missouri sang, "We'll hang John Brown to a sour apple tree."

Most of the Kansans, even though they might not approve of the Pottawatomie murders, respected John Brown's sincerity and selflessness. On the other hand, there were those

who did not take such a lenient view of his activities. Among
the latter was William Clarke Quantrill, better known as
Charley Quantrill, the bloody avenger whose name rang up
and down the Missouri border during the war, when he was
the leader of a band of Missouri guerillas.

Quantrill was a Kansan, who had come in 1857 from the
town of Canol Dover, Ohio. He was of medium build, with a
large head set on a rather thin neck, and almost white hair,
a high forehead, large, heavy-lidded blue-gray eyes, a round,
heavy face, and a detached, if not sardonic, expression. He
was a member of the Free State party, and ostensibly a Free
State man until late in 1860 when he transferred his operations to Missouri. However, in private letters to his family
in Ohio as early as January of 1860, he was writing disparag-
ingly of his fellow Kansans. "They all sympathize with Old
John Brown," he wrote. "A murderer and a robber made a
martyr of; just think of it." In February he wrote: "The Devil
has got unlimited sway over this country."

In his divided state of mind, Quantrill began trafficking
with both the proslavery and antislavery elements at Lawrence. He told each group that he was spying on the other.
One day he would be going on a raid into Missouri to free
Negroes; the next night he would be kidnaping Negroes to
return them to their owners, for the $200 statutory reward
offered for runaways. Presently he was under suspicion from
both sides. Seasoned abolitionists no longer would go on raids
into Missouri if Quantrill was in the party—they didn't trust
him. Then warrants were issued charging Quantrill with kidnaping and with stealing horses from a near-by Indian res-
ervation. Kansas was getting to be highly unsafe for him.

For the purpose of transferring himself to the Missouri side,
he hit upon a treacherous plan. In mid-December of 1860, he
persuaded three innocent and newly arrived Quakers from

Iowa to go on a raid with him. He told them they could easily
liberate slaves from the farm of Morgan Walker, who lived
seven miles southeast of Independence. Walker, farming two
thousand acres, had thirty-two slaves and more than one-
hundred horses and mules.

Quantrill and the Quakers walked into Missouri. As they
approached the Walker farm, Quantrill went ahead, ostensibly to reconnoiter. Actually, he knocked on the Walkers'
door, warned them that there would be a raid on their place
that night, and helped them lay plans to kill his companions.
The Walkers in exchange agreed to receive Quantrill safely
into their house. He then returned to his companions, and that
night led them to their doom. They walked up to the Walkers'
front door, and Quantrill entered the house, after the approved fashion for such raids. The slaveowners were usually
held at gun point while the Negroes harnessed animals to
wagons and started for the border. Since the border was
usually only ten or fifteen miles away, they would be safe in
Kansas before effective pursuit could be organized. But on
this occasion, Quantrill by pre-arrangement remained in the
Walker home; while his companions were killed by Walker's
neighbors, who were waiting with shotguns and rifles in the
bushes outside.

Quantrill's position in Missouri was not immediately secure.
The Missourians regarded him as a "Jayhawker," and saw
nothing extenuating in the fact that he had betrayed his
companions. He was arrested and jailed at Independence. A
son of Morgan Walker, Andrew J. Walker, defended him
and obtained his release from jail, only to learn that a large
crowd had gathered in the Independence square with the
intention of hanging Quantrill. Walker made an impassioned
plea from the courthouse steps, and the crowd desisted from
its intention. But people still looked suspiciously on Quantrill

and on advice of the Walkers he left that part of the country for a time.

Soon afterward the organized fighting of the Civil War began. A report was circulated that Quantrill had fought gallantly with the Confederates in the Battle of Wilson Creek. He returned to the Walkers in October, 1861. Federal troops had established several garrisons in the county, and the month of Quantrill's return a Federal soldier was killed while foraging in the Walker vicinity. Two landowners were accused of his murder. Quantrill executed an affidavit that he had done the killing, and the landowners were freed. This action further helped him to gain the confidence of the Missouri countryside, but at the same time it made him an outlaw to the Federal troops. He collected a guerilla band around him and managed to elude capture for the rest of the war. Quantrill, a Kansan, thus became the leader of the far-famed Missouri guerillas. However shaky his background, it could not be denied that his men swore by him both during and after the war, and that in fighting with a small, irregular force, he had scarcely an equal.

Excepting Quantrill, the Missouri guerillas were nearly all Missourians, operating close to their homes. Frank and Jesse James, later more widely known as outlaws, came from a farm north of the Missouri River. Cole Younger, also later with the same outlaw band, was from south of the river. Frank James was with Quantrill during most of the war. Jesse James, as a youth of seventeen, joined the guerillas toward the close of the war—in time, however, to see some fierce action. Cole Younger had a separate guerilla band which hung on the outskirts of Kansas City, but Younger's band frequently joined forces with Quantrill's. Another separate band was maintained by "Bloody Bill" Anderson, whose deeds matched those of Quantrill.

In general, the guerillas were the sons of landowners. Cole Younger's father was Colonel Henry M. Younger, who had been among the early settlers in Jackson County and had been mentioned as serving as a camp aide to Washington Irving when the writer passed through the Kansas City region in 1832, gathering material for his *Tour of the Prairies*. Colonel Younger later served a term as a Jackson County judge and three terms in the state legislature. He owned two large farms, kept a store and livery stable, possessed slaves and held a franchise for a mail contract extending some five hundred miles, with stables of horses along the route. He reported that he had lost twenty thousand dollars' worth of horses and vehicles to the Kansas Jayhawkers.

When all of the guerilla bands were together, they numbered about three hundred well-mounted men. Quantrill's own force comprised approximately one hundred horsemen. They were known as the "Bushwhackers," because they inhabited the brush, and all of them were based in the immediate environs of Kansas City.

Missouri from the beginning was an outpost state for the South, and the loss of Kansas left it in an even more exposed position. Free Illinois was on the east, free Iowa on the north and free Kansas on the west. Only Arkansas on the south and its boot-heel frontier with Kentucky and Tennessee connected Missouri with the other Southern States. During the Civil War, Federal troops easily entered Kansas City from Kansas and St. Louis from Illinois.

St. Louis between 1848 and 1860 had received so much German and Irish immigration that its population was 60 per cent foreign born, and that city largely sided with the North. The remainder of the state had been little affected by the overseas immigration of the period, but outlying sections contained large pro-Northern or pro-Union elements. Even in the central portion of the state, in the rich river counties, there were many who, like Benton, were Southern in origin and sympathy, but who did not favor secession. After the outbreak of war, Missouri's elected governor moved to the South; its acting governor was a provisional appointee of the United States Government; its representatives sat in the congresses of both sides. The state offered a patchwork of conflicting loyalties that was often baffling both to the North and to the South.

The real key to the situation lay in whether Union or Confederate armies would be able to maintain themselves on Missouri soil. In this, the Union forces proved much more successful. Federal troops occupied the principal towns and cities, and kept open the navigation of the Missouri River except for short periods of time. In the end Missouri furnished more troops to the North than to the South. Each year during the war, Confederate armies pushed into southern Missouri, at times reaching the river and holding approximately half the state; but each year they were driven back into Arkansas. The only portion of Missouri which the Federal troops were never able to control was the rural section immediately around Kansas City, where Charley Quantrill and his bold guerillas relentlessly held sway.

Although Kansas City had served as a landing and transfer point for the Kansas settlers, the city's own population had remained largely Southern in origin. Of its five or six thousand residents in 1860, only seventy-two voted for Abraham Lincoln; and the names of these voters were prominently posted as a blacklist on the courthouse door in Independence. During the early part of 1861 when the Southern States were seceding, Confederate sympathizers staged a big parade through the streets of the city, and ran up the rebel flag in the market square. Secession flags flew from many Kansas City windows, one man counting thirteen in his block.

However, the city was not as Southern as the Missouri countryside. It did not have large slave interests, and it did have extensive commercial connections with the North and West. So the city divided sharply on the issue of secession, and after some maneuvering elected a pro-Union man, Robert T. Van Horn, to succeed its pro-Southern mayor. Mayor Van Horn called in Federal troops from Leavenworth for protection. He expelled the pro-Southern police force, and organized Union militia. Kansas City thus became a headquarters for Federal troops, many of them Kansans. Independence had strong Confederate sympathies; but once established in Kansas City the Union troops moved into Independence and, after some skirmishing, garrisoned it with six hundred men. They also garrisoned Westport and the smaller towns of Pink Hill, Lone Jack, Stoney Point, and Sibley. In between and on the edges of these garrisons were Quantrill's Bushwhackers. At times the Bushwhackers even held the ten-mile stretch of road between Independence and Kansas City. In one week on that road, on successive days, they captured six horsemen who were attempting to bring mail into the city. Sometimes the guerillas entered Kansas City, Westport, and Independence in disguise or in raiding parties.

Since the Bushwhackers numbered only three hundred men, and there were thousands of Federal troops available to pursue them, it would seem that the Bushwhackers should have been quickly exterminated. But the guerillas of those days, like their counterparts in later times, proved to be elusive. When a small Federal detachment ventured forth from the garrisoned towns, the detachment was in imminent danger. When a large Union force went out to hunt the Bushwhackers, the guerillas hid in the brush, of which there was plenty. General Thomas E. Ewing, when he was Federal commander at Kansas City with six or seven thousand troops at his disposal, reported that during the full-leaf season it was impossible to hunt down the guerillas, however few they might be—and in the winter season, when the trees and brush were bare, Quantrill and his men went south into Arkansas or Texas.

Two-thirds of the country people had relatives either among the guerillas or among the men in the regular Confederate service, so the guerillas did not lack for food and other local support. The Southerners who gave such aid did so quietly, not wishing to incur Federal reprisals. Colonel Jennison and his Kansas command often rode across the border to burn the homes and plunder the livestock of families reported to have aided Quantrill. Nevertheless, later accounts of Quantrill's movements mention stops at such prominent homes as that of Alexander Majors, who, before the war, had operated one of the largest of the wagon-freighting outfits, and had started the Pony Express. "He (Quantrill) camped always in or near a large house," wrote one of his men, giving tactical reasons for this procedure. The activity of the guerillas was the principal reason for Kansas City's commercial decline during the war, since the routes to the city became unsafe. They also made the countryside dangerous for such avowed pro-Union men as might wish to oppose them, and most of the pro-Union families moved for protection into the garrisoned towns.

CHAPTER FOUR

Order No. 11

IN MAY, 1863, the trees and brush were in full leaf, and the Bushwhackers of the countryside were in full activity. A guerilla named Jim Vaughan, disguised in a captured Federal uniform, decided he could safely enter Kansas City to get a shave and a haircut. Unfortunately for Vaughan, while the razor was poised over him and escape was most difficult, he was recognized by a pro-Union man and was taken prisoner by Federal troops. The ban of outlawry had been pronounced against the guerillas; parties hunting them often carried black flags to indicate that no quarter would be given them; and they were subject to the death penalty if caught. It was determined that Vaughan should be publicly hanged.

Quantrill hastily rounded up three fairly important Federal prisoners, a lieutenant, an orderly and a private, and offered to exchange them for Vaughan. The guerilla leader even adopted the unusual procedure of sending the lieutenant on his honor into Kansas City, to plead for his own exchange. But it was to no avail. The Federal officers in this case took the position that they could not deal with pro-Southern guerillas whom the Confederacy itself at times was reluctant to recognize. So the execution was carried out. As he stood on the scaffold, Vaughan said: "We can be killed but we cannot be conquered. Taking my life today will cost you one hundred lives, and this debt my friends will pay in a very short time."

Soon afterward, on June 17, 1863, a group of fifty or sixty mounted guerillas saw a company of Federal cavalry crossing the Kansas prairie toward Westport. The guerillas entered Westport on the south, followed the timber along Brush Creek, and concealed themselves and their horses along a lane which had a high rock fence on either side. Suspecting nothing, the Federals rode carelessly into this enclosed lane, the captain with one leg thrown over his horse's neck. The guerillas then charged down upon them, and threw them into a panic. Some were killed in the lane, and the rest were pursued back onto the prairie. The attackers were left temporarily in possession of the field, where they counted thirty-three Federal dead, as against three dead of their own. One guerilla wrote on a slip of paper, "Remember the dying words of Jim Vaughan," and placed the note between the teeth of a dead Federal officer. This action was followed by a number of lesser skirmishes, and before long, as Vaughan had predicted on the scaffold, the debt of one hundred lives had been paid.

While the feeling over these episodes was running high, a number of Confederate young women, especially girls who were related to guerillas, were taken into custody and brought to Kansas City. The Federal command was determined that these girls should no longer be permitted to supply food and give information to the Bushwhackers. Some of the girls were arrested when they brought loads of wheat in oxcarts into town to exchange for flour and other provisions, and others

were taken in their homes. The Bushwhackers had until
then been getting their ammunition through connections in
Kansas City, and that traffic had been stopped; now it was
proposed to cut off the balance of their supplies.

Because of the arrest of so many women, they could not all
be accommodated in the Union Hotel, ordinarily used for
women prisoners. Other quarters were needed for seventeen
girls. A three-story brick building between Fourteenth and
Fifteenth on Grand was selected. The building was the
property of George Caleb Bingham, the successful and widely
known Missouri artist. Bingham was not using the structure
—he was away serving a term as State Treasurer at Jefferson
City—and the upper two stories were vacant.

On the first floor was a grocery store; the second floor contained living quarters, and the third had formerly been used
by the artist as his studio. The girls were housed on the second
and third floors, and a Kansas sergeant was placed in charge
of the guards. The sergeant permitted the girls to go to the
stores under guard, instructing the guards to remain far
enough behind them so as not to overhear their conversation;
in general, he appears to have treated them as well as, or better
than, prisoners were usually treated. That the conditions of
imprisonment were not considered onerous was shown by the
fact that, after Josephine and Mary Anderson were arrested,
their ten-year-old sister Janie came in voluntarily to live with
them. The child was permitted to stay, and was given the
same consideration as the other girls.

Nevertheless, there was negligence in the selection of the
building in which these girls were housed. The cause of its
structural weakness was never conclusively determined, although there was endless discussion on the subject. It was
pointed out that the rear of the building extended into a
ravine, and that there the walls of the foundation had been

built without excavation. Plans had been made to fill in the ravine, and thus give the back part of the foundation greater earth support; but these plans had not been carried out. The rear room of the building had not been completed, and hogs which still ranged at large in Kansas City had come there to lie in the shade and to root in the loose earth, no doubt knocking against the foundation walls and contributing to the building's instability. Further, General Bingham, as the artist was called after serving a term as the state's Adjutant General, had added the third floor for his studio sometime after the first two stories were completed. Since the original design was for a two-story structure, the additional weight may have been too great for the foundation.

In any case, two or three weeks after he was placed in charge of the guards, the Kansas sergeant reported that he did not think the building was safe. He said it appeared to be cracking at the seams. An army inspector was sent out, and on his arrival found that the Jewish storekeeper who occupied the first floor was moving his merchandise into the street in the expectation that the building might fall. But the cracks that had alarmed the sergeant and the storekeeper failed to impress the inspector. After standing around for a while, first on one foot and then the other, with a generally careless attitude toward the whole affair, he reported that the building was safe.

The next morning the building collapsed. Its walls fell inward, raising a great cloud of dust. In that day there was no steel framework in buildings, and the girls were buried under a crushing pile of brick and mortar which thundered down into the ravine. Four of the girls, all related to guerillas, were killed outright. Several were seriously injured.

During the frantic period when the girls still living were being dug out, a crowd of three or four thousand people gathered. The crowd showed much angry hostility toward the guards and sympathy for the girls. A report circulated that the foundation had been deliberately undermined in order to murder the girls. Although the collapse of the building undoubtedly was the result of gross negligence rather than deliberate intent, the belief that it was deliberate was widely held then, as well as fifty years later. The guerillas were fully convinced that the girls had been murdered. Under the standards prevailing during the Civil War, women on both sides were usually treated with respect—there seems to have been no complaint against the guerillas on this score—and the incident assumed greater importance than would be indicated by the number of dead.

One of the bodies taken from the wreckage was that of Mrs. Charity Kerr, a sister of Quantrill's chief scout, John McCorkle, and a cousin of Cole Younger. Another of the dead was Josephine Anderson, a sister of Bloody Bill Anderson. Bloody Bill, second or third to Quantrill in public notoriety, thereafter carried in his pocket a silken cord in which eventually he tied fifty-three knots, the knots serving the same purpose as notches on a gun. The summer of that year, some of the guerillas began taking scalps, displaying them as trophies dangling from their saddle horns. And in the days immediately following the collapse of the building, they planned the Lawrence massacre. The building collapsed on August 13, 1863, and the Lawrence massacre occurred on August 21, 1863. "You can get more revenge in Lawrence than anywhere else," declared Quantrill; and "Lawrence it is," agreed Anderson.

For the Lawrence raid all the guerilla bands, for the first time, were gathered together. There were two hundred and ninety-four horsemen. Two small Confederate commands, that were recruiting in the vicinity, accompanied them on the raid. The total in the party that started for Lawrence was four hundred and forty-eight men. Most of them were in a blood-thirsty mood. In addition to the events in Kansas City, there was the knowledge that many Southern homes in Jackson County had been burned by Kansas raiders, and by parties of Federal "regulators" sent through the rural districts. Chimneys built for kitchen fireplaces stood solemnly amid the ruins of these homes, and in many cases the Southern families were living in shacks nearby. Lawrence was the home of Senator James H. Lane, considered to be the chief of the Kansas raiders; and the guerillas had plans for bringing Lane back alive and hanging him publicly.

The Bushwhackers and their companions entered Kansas at a point below Kansas City, in midafternoon of August 20. They carried a death list of intended victims, including Lane and all who had taken part with him in the earlier burning of the town of Osceola, Missouri—a raid in which one person was killed. The first name on their death list was a Colonel Sims, a Missourian who had been an active "Benton Democrat," and antislavery man, and who had moved into Kansas. They stopped near Squireville, Kansas, and hammered on Colonel Sims' door. Fortunately for the colonel, he was not at home. The four hundred and forty-eight horsemen proceeded to Gardner, Kansas, then a village on the Santa Fé Trail. They reached Gardner at 11:00 P.M., having completed about half of their forty-mile journey to Lawrence.

Beyond Gardner, they began to need the services of a guide. The moon had gone down, and there was only starlight. Although Quantrill had lived at Lawrence, the intervening country here was badly cut up by creeks, and in the semi-darkness he was not sure of his ground. The Bushwhackers adopted the practice of routing Kansas farmers from their beds to act as guides. These farmers were used as long as they were of service, and then were shot. According to William H. Gregg, one of Quantrill's captains, at least ten guides were shot in this fashion during the move on Lawrence.

Just at daybreak on August 21, the Bushwhackers, wearing low-crowned, broad-brimmed hats, and for the most part unshaven and clad in red flannel shirts, came within sight of Lawrence and broke their horses into a gallop.

A number of people knew that the Bushwhackers were moving on Lawrence, and several had started to warn the town. For one reason or another, none of these warnings reached Lawrence. The guerillas moved rapidly over the country, and there was no way of sending information ahead except by horse. When the enemy charged down upon them, most of the citizens of Lawrence were in their beds. Before they knew what was happening, the Bushwhackers had scattered through the town. "Remember the murdered girls in Kansas City," was one of the cries raised in the streets of Lawrence.

The orders from Quantrill, as generally reported, were to shoot every man who could carry a gun. If those were the orders, they were not fully carried out; even Quantrill protected a number of male prisoners. But a great many victims were trapped in their homes, and shot, after which their houses were burned. Some of these men died because they were on the death list, and some simply because they were there. Bloody Bill Anderson tied fourteen knots in his silken cord, and he was not particular how he accumulated that number.

Most of the accounts place the number of dead in the Lawrence massacre at one hundred and fifty. Seventeen of these were raw Federal recruits and six or eight were Federal soldiers on leave; the rest were civilians. In numbers of civilians killed, nothing comparable occurred either in Kansas or

Missouri, either before or during the war. The Bushwhackers were in Lawrence four hours. In that time they burned two hundred houses, all but one hotel, and all but two business buildings. They left eighty widows, and two hundred and fifty orphans. The loss in destruction and in loot carried away was officially placed at $882,000.

The Bushwhackers' principal quarry at Lawrence, James H. Lane, escaped them. Lane, a general in the Union Army and a United States Senator, famous in Kansas and infamous in Missouri, started from his bed as soon as he heard shooting. He ran in his nightshirt across lots until he reached a field of full-grown corn. Then he followed a ravine to a farmhouse, where he borrowed a pair of oversized trousers. He pulled the trousers up over the tails of his nightshirt, borrowed a work horse with a blind bridle and, thus attired and mounted, rounded up a party of a dozen or so farmers in time to pursue the guerillas back into Missouri.

Quantrill and his men fled Lawrence upon the approach of Federal troops, who had been attracted from near-by points by the burning of the town. These troops also pursued them, and the guerillas fought rear-guard actions all the way back to the border. Hard pressed though they were, and two nights without sleep, they escaped, and scattered into their haunts in Missouri. The tall, thin Senator Lane of Kansas, still wearing his nightshirt and borrowed trousers, entered Kansas City. He was a man of much influence with the War Department in Washington, and he was determined to prevent the possibility of further guerilla raids into Kansas. He therefore demanded immediate and drastic action to depopulate the rural sections of Jackson and adjacent counties, a demand that resulted in Order No. 11. General Thomas E. Ewing, the Federal commander of the Kansas City military district, always defended this order as his own; but, according to the

Kansas historian W. E. Connelley, he issued it at Senator Lane's insistence. The joint contention of General Ewing and Senator Lane was that raiding could not be stopped while the guerillas had both cover and the support of the population; since they could not remove the cover, they would remove the population.

Ewing's General Order No. 11 was posted August 25, 1863, four days after the Lawrence massacre. All the rural people of Jackson and two other counties were required to move from their farms within fifteen days. If they would take an oath of loyalty to the Union, they were permitted to move into the garrisoned towns, or into districts within one mile of these towns; if they would not take such an oath, they were obliged to move into the interior of Missouri. In either case they could not remain in their homes. Federal troops deployed over the countryside to enforce the order, and lines of refugees with baggage-laden wagons filed into the towns and into the interior counties. Approximately twenty thousand people were moved off the land. A second section of Order No. 11 directed the troops to destroy all grain and hay remaining on farms after the fifteen-day period, the purpose being to prevent the guerillas from feeding their horses. The flames of burning barns and haystacks, and sometimes burning houses, lighted the countryside at night.

The order aroused lasting resentment in border Missouri. For every wrong committed in Kansas, the Missourians cited one committed in Missouri by the Kansas Jayhawkers, or the "Red Legs" as they came to be called (because certain of the Kansas scouts wore red sheepskin leggings). Guerillas who had been at Lawrence claimed that in Senator Lane's parlor they had seen two "thousand dollar pianos" that had been stolen from Missouri, and they gave many other accounts of Missouri property carried into Kansas. This property loss was

greatly increased where Order No. 11 went into effect. Not
all of the farmers' hay, grain, and equipment could be loaded
into wagons and hauled off in fifteen days, nor could all their
livestock be taken. According to the accounts of later years, a
motley assortment of speculators, shysters, and moneygrub-
bers scoured over the land in the wake of the retreating
population, some of them making small fortunes by rounding
up stray cattle and whatever else they could find that was of
value.

At the time Order No. 11 was issued, the artist George Caleb
Bingham was in Jefferson City, serving as State Treasurer. A
fiery personality, he was outraged by the order and posted
with all speed back to Kansas City. As the owner of the building that had collapsed, he was himself partly involved, and he
blamed the Federal command for its negligence in that incident. Upon reaching Kansas City, Bingham went immediately to General Ewing at the Federal headquarters in the
Pacific House and threatened, if the order was not withdrawn
upon the instant, to make the general "infamous with pen
and brush."

Bingham was a Union and an antislavery man, a long-time
admirer of Senator Benton, and a captain in Kansas City's
Union militia; and he had often condemned the guerillas. Yet
he was a Missourian and a Southerner, and during the war he
frequently was the champion of the Southern element in
attacks on the Kansas raiders, whom he denounced as "the
Red Legs and their equally demoniac associates, known only
as thieves and assassins." He was especially vehement in his
attacks upon Colonel Jennison, the most active of the Kansas
raiders. In a celebrated controversy he brought charges of
burning and robbery which caused the War Department to
deprive Jennison temporarily of military rank. Bingham's
standing as a Union man, combined with his sympathies for

those wronged by either side, made him the logical man to
lead the protest against Order No. 11.

He stirred up such a protest that after a few months General
Ewing was in effect removed, through a typical War Department maneuver. The Kansas City military department was
technically abolished, the administration of the area was
attached to the Federal headquarters at Leavenworth, Kansas, and Ewing was assigned to another post. A limited
number of persons was then allowed to return to the land. But
as long as he was in command, General Ewing defended his
order in full. He never conceded that there were people in the
rural districts who were not aiding the Bushwhackers. "All
the people of the country, through fear or favor, fed them," he
reported. On the other hand, Missourians regarded Order No.
11 as an inhuman exaction of revenge on a defenseless population. They viewed Order No. 11 with its consequent destruction in the same light as the South viewed Sherman's
march to the sea. *

There was no official report of any deaths caused in ex-
ecuting Order No. 11, but Bingham said he personally knew
of farmers being shot down by the enforcing troops while in
the very act of obeying the order. He declared he would "hand
over to eternal infamy the perpetrators and defenders of outrages which scarcely find a parallel in the annals of the most
barbarous ages." This he proceeded to do by speaking and
writing against the order, and by painting *Order No. 11*, the
most famous painting of the Civil War in the West.†

In the painting, he showed a likeness of General Ewing
astride a horse, directing the expulsion of a Southern family.
One Red Leg has just shot down a young man, and another is

---

* General Sherman and General Ewing, incidentally, were foster brothers,
brought up in the same household.

† The painting *Order No. 11* hangs in the reading room of the State Historical Society of Missouri, at Columbia, Mo.

about to shoot the gray-haired protesting head of the house. Other members of the family are in various attitudes of flight and fright, while in the background are the fires and smoke of burning hay and grain, and a long, funereal line of refugees.

Least affected by Order No. 11 were the Bushwhackers, against whom it was directed. The guerillas rode far, and had friends in many places. By one means or another, they continued to supply themselves, and although the countryside was desolated they continued to frequent their haunts around Kansas City. They were at least as strong in 1864 as they had been in 1863. Subsequent to Order No. 11 occurred both of the battles for which the guerillas, as a fighting unit, were chiefly remembered. The order did cause them to go south a little earlier than usual in the fall of 1863; and this in turn brought them into position for the first of the two battles, which was fought October 6, 1863, outside of Baxter Springs, a town in southern Kansas near the Missouri border.

Quantrill and a column of about one hundred guerillas were riding southward along the Missouri-Kansas border, en route to Texas, when they encountered the Kansas General, James G. Blunt. General Blunt on this day was not looking for a fight, but was rather on a military inspection tour. He was riding in a carriage behind a pair of beautiful dun horses with docked tails, and beside him on the seat of the carriage was a five-gallon demijohn of brandy, with which to treat his friends. With him was a mounted bodyguard of two hundred men. The guerillas charged this bodyguard before Blunt could organize a defense. Blunt's men turned to run for it, and the battle almost immediately became a pursuit, which continued for a quarter of a mile to the banks of a deep ravine which many of the horses would not take, and where the greatest slaughter

occurred. As Frank James remembered in later years, there
were one hundred and thirty Federal dead on the Baxter
Springs field that day. The official report was eighty killed
and eighteen wounded. The guerillas lost only two killed and
two wounded.

The second long-remembered guerilla charge was made on
September 27, 1864. This was the time of year for General
Sterling Price and his Missouri-Arkansas Confederates to
conduct their "annual" invasion of southern Missouri. When
the regular Confederate troops entered the state, the guerillas
usually tried to join them, and to "cut in" on the regular fighting. For the purpose of joining the Confederates, Quantrill
and his men had followed the back roads and the timber along
streams until they reached central Missouri. They then received orders to go north of the river and create a diversion,
which might help the troops that were fighting farther south.
The action, therefore, occurred in central Missouri, north of
the river.

Preceding the battle, on the morning of September 27,
Bloody Bill Anderson with eighty men entered Centralia,
Missouri, a railroad town with less than one hundred inhabitants. Anderson's men stopped the first passenger train
coming through by placing ties on the track and, boarding the
train, captured twenty-three Federal soldiers, most of whom
were on furlough. The guerillas set fire to the train and depot,
and plundered the two Centralia stores. Then on Anderson's
order they executed before a firing squad twenty-two of the
twenty-three captured Federals, sparing only one sergeant
for exchange purposes. Except for the Lawrence massacre,
this was the most infamous guerilla action of the war, and it
disturbed Union troops in far corners of the country, because
the executed men were clearly entitled to treatment as
prisoners.

Two hours later, Major A. V. E. Johnson of the Thirty-ninth Missouri Infantry reached Centralia with a Union force of 206 mounted infantrymen. He set forth in pursuit of the guerillas. Anderson's band had withdrawn to a point three miles from Centralia, where they had been joined by Quantrill's men and several lesser bands. There were 264 horsemen in the guerilla camp. They outnumbered Johnson's men, and they were much more experienced in fighting. Presently the two forces were in full view of each other, across a stretch of prairie. Major Johnson ordered his men to dismount, detailed every fourth man to hold horses, and placed the balance in rifle positions along the crest of the slope. He then faced the guerillas with a line of approximately 150 riflemen on foot, in the day of the single-shot rifle.

Southerners in general were supremely confident of the superiority of horsemen over foot soldiers, and the guerillas saw Johnson's maneuvers with amazement. "The fools; they're going to fight us on foot," someone called. "God help them," was the word that passed along the guerilla line as they mounted for the charge. They rode their horses low, after the fashion of the Comanche Indians; and they relied almost altogether on their revolvers, holding their fire until they were within six or eight feet of the enemy. By hanging on their horses' necks, they largely protected themselves from opposing bullets, and their own shots were usually fatal.

The charging guerillas, spread out over a half mile, were still more than one hundred yards away and were converging when Johnson's men fired for the first and only time. Only two attacking horsemen fell; nearly all the bullets were over their heads. When the guerillas reached the Federal line, some of Johnson's men were at fixed bayonets, some were biting off cartridges in an effort to re-load, and some seemed hypnotized. Not a man in the line escaped; all were killed on the spot, and according to later testimony all were shot in the head. Among those detailed to hold horses, only fourteen escaped, and two of these were seriously wounded. The guerilla casualties at Centralia were three dead, including one who died later of lockjaw.

Frank and Jesse James fought together in the Battle of Centralia. Jesse James, then seventeen, had joined Bloody Bill Anderson's band, and was known to his companions as "Dingus." Up to a few months before, he had not learned the art of profanity, and while struggling with a saddle girth was heard to exclaim, "This is the dad-dingest thing I ever saw!" thus acquiring his nickname. By the time of Centralia, however, he was a full-fledged fighting man. According to the accounts of Frank James and others, young Jesse James himself fired the bullet that killed Major Johnson.

In creating the diversion, the guerillas spent two weeks north of the Missouri River, and engaged a number of Federal troop units. They estimated that they had killed one thousand Federal soldiers. At the end of the two weeks, the Confederates under General Price had fought their way northward to the river. The guerillas therefore withdrew southward to the river, and at Booneville, Missouri, they joined the regular Confederates for an advance on Kansas City.

General Sterling Price was a former Missouri governor, and originally was a Union man, in the sense that he believed there should be a federal union of the states. He was, in fact, the president of a Missouri convention which on February 28, 1861, had decided *not* to secede. However, General Price's conception of states' rights was such that an action by Federal troops to protect a United States arsenal could be

Senator Thomas Hart Benton

Kansas Landing from an old print

construed as an act of aggression. Incidents occurred almost immediately with the outbreak of the war, and General Price from the first fought against Federal troops. For nearly a year he fought under the flag of Missouri. Then he hoisted the Confederate flag and was placed in command of the Confederate Army of the West. These Missouri-Arkansas troops under General Price did most of the fighting for the Confederacy that occurred beyond the Mississippi.

During the Civil War it was a common remark among Missourians that the seasons might be referred to as spring, summer, Price's raid and winter; and at all seasons rumors of his coming abounded. In 1864, when General Price came northward for the third and last time, he had the most powerful mobile force he had yet assembled. He had ten thousand seasoned horsemen, a baggage train of five hundred wagons, eight twenty-pounder guns, and a large number of twelve-pounder mountain howitzers. As he fought his way northward, he pressed an additional six thousand men into service.

General Price was attached to Missouri's elected and fugitive state government; or rather, the fugitive government was attached to him. His principal objective in 1864 was Jefferson City, the Missouri State Capital, located on the Missouri River near the center of the state. He had high hopes of capturing the city and there seating his Confederate government. Price therefore only feinted toward St. Louis on the east and then proceeded to Jefferson City.

However, upon reaching the capital's edge, he decided that the city was too strongly held, and that an attack would be useless. He camped on a rise overlooking Jefferson City only long enough to allow his long baggage train to pass around the city, and then moved westward. The only logical objective to the west for such a force was Kansas City, which in turn could be used as a base for an attack on Fort Leavenworth in Kansas. General Price publicly announced that he intended to take both these cities.

The Kansas City military department having been abolished, Major General Samuel R. Curtis of Fort Leavenworth was the Federal commander for both places. He arranged the defense of Kansas City. The populations of both Kansas City and Westport were called out to dig trenches and throw up breastworks in front of the two towns. Many residents buried their valuables in the expectation that the city would be captured. Martial law was declared in the state of Kansas, and every man there who could carry a gun was called up. The settlers from the Kansas farms poured into Kansas City, carrying frying pans, packages of bread and bacon, rifles and shotguns.

All told, including experienced troops and raw recruits, General Curtis assembled fifteen thousand men for the defense of Kansas City. Most of them were Kansans, and many of these Kansans objected to being stationed in Missouri, even though Kansas City was the recognized doorstep to Kansas. General Curtis found it necessary to place a brigadier general and a colonel under arrest because they so vigorously contended he had no authority to take troops out of the state; and one regiment of the highly democratic Kansas army, almost on the eve of battle, held an election to select a new colonel. Because of the frequent false rumors of his coming, there were many assertions that General Price would never reach Kansas City, and that he had probably left the state, "if he had ever entered it." General Curtis was even accused of manufacturing the incident, and of calling up troops in an effort to influence a forthcoming Kansas election. Nevertheless, the Kansans constituted a brave and effective fighting force. Not least among them were General Blunt, whom

Quantrill had once defeated, and Colonel Jennison, the raider who had aroused the ire of the Missourians.

On October 21, 1864, General Curtis with a delaying force met Price and his advancing Confederates on the Little Blue River, flowing eight miles east of Independence. In a sharp action, the Confederates easily drove back the Federal vanguard and took Independence. On the following day, October 22, the Confederates forced a crossing of the Big Blue River, flowing between Independence and Kansas City. With their famous Missouri cavalry leading the way, they drove under heavy Federal fire through timbers that had been thrown in to clog the Big Blue's fords. This broke the main Federal line of defense, and threw the defenders behind the breastworks in front of Kansas City and Westport.

However, in achieving the major break, the Confederates had felt obliged to veer toward the south, in order to keep the southward route open for retreat if necessary. Their line, strung all the way from Independence, was not pointed directly at Kansas City, but rather at Westport. After the break, Colonel Jennison and a force of Kansans fell back to Westport, and conducted a successful defense. The Confederates were lodged for the night in the timber on the south side of Brush Creek, which flows through the Westport section. They were four miles from the outskirts of the then small Kansas City.

A major factor in the Confederate considerations was that they were also being pursued. When General Price passed Jefferson City, Major General Alfred Pleasonton had set out in pursuit from that place, with sixty-five hundred men. Now, at the crucial moment before Kansas City, this Federal force was driving in upon the Confederate rear. Scarcely two hours after the Confederates crossed the Big Blue, the pursuing Federals caught and attacked their rear in Independence.

The Confederate rear guard then withdrew to the Big Blue, where they took up the positions the Kansans had formerly held in defending that line. The Confederates were then attacking before Westport, and also fighting a rear-guard action on the Big Blue. This was the situation as the day closed on October 22.

The next morning, October 23, General Curtis and his Kansans attacked the Confederates in the timber on the south side of Brush Creek. The Kansans charged up a ravine, beginning a few hundred yards west of where Wornall Road crosses the creek, and turned Price's left flank. The Confederates were forced gradually to withdraw from the timber. At the same time, the pursuing Federals were attacking the Confederate rear guard on the Big Blue. The two battlefields were about to become one.

The pursuers were mostly Union Missourians, with some troops from Illinois, but they included also a famous Kansas regiment—the Seventh Kansas, known as the Jayhawkers. One of its captains was John Brown, Jr. Captain Brown was accustomed to lecturing his men, and to ending his speeches with, "Do you solemnly swear to avenge the death of John Brown?" To which the audience would respond with, "We do." The fighting temper of the regiment was well known, and the rest of the pursuers were also seasoned men. After exchanging fire with the Confederates for several hours, they charged across the Big Blue on a half-mile front just north of the present Swope Park. With a mighty cheer, they reached the high ground on the other side, pushed back the Confederate rear guard, and advanced to join General Curtis and his Kansans. At exactly noon on October 23, General Curtis heard the approaching guns of Pleasonton's force, and knew that the battle was as good as won. He dispatched a horseman into Kansas City with a message to that effect, and in the midst of battle began mustering out some of his least useful Kansans.

General Price had detached a portion of his men to start his cumbersome wagon train moving southward, and he had only nine thousand Confederates on the field. With the accretion of the pursuers, the Union troops faced them with twenty thousand men, on a battlefield covering four square miles. The Confederates continued to fight from behind a large number of stone fences that had been built around fields, but they were gradually forced back. The fighting was viewed from the housetops in Kansas City, and the wounded were brought to Kansas City and Westport homes. Casualties were estimated at one thousand, in killed and wounded for both sides.

This was the largest and most decisive battle fought west of the Mississippi during the Civil War. It became known as the Battle of Westport, and as the "Gettysburg of the West." Much of the action took place on ground that today is Loose Park in Kansas City. As in the case of the Battle of Gettysburg, the Battle of Westport broke the power of the Confederacy to conduct aggressive warfare in a section of the country, and it destroyed the attackers as a fighting unit. The Confederates were able to retreat from Westport, but two days later were overtaken at Mound City, Kansas, near the border. Hard pressed by the pursuit, they exploded their reserve ammunition and burned their wagon train. On Mine Creek near Mound City, eight hundred Confederates were taken prisoners and the rest scattered, Price himself escaping, thanks only to a good horse. "Everything is now a mass of confusion and the morale of the army is ruined," wrote Price's adjutant on October 25.

Much Missouri personal history was telescoped in those hours of fighting before Westport. Price's van was led by

Brigadier General Jo (Joseph O.) Shelby, one of Missouri's principal Confederate heroes and a future political power in the state. Price's rear guard was under the command of Major General J. S. Marmaduke, a future Missouri governor. The Union Missourians who spearheaded the great drive across the Big Blue were led by Colonel John F. Philips, later a Federal judge in Kansas City; and Thomas T. Crittenden, another future governor, was among the Union Missourians wounded.

The Battle of Westport was the last great onslaught for the guerillas. Quantrill's second in command, Captain George Todd, was killed in the fighting at Independence, and Bloody Bill Anderson was fatally shot during a side skirmish in Ray County. Thus two of the three principal guerilla leaders died in the course of the advance upon Kansas City. Quantrill himself lived several more months, and then was killed in a skirmish that occurred when he conducted his band on a strange eastward foray into Kentucky. According to some accounts, Quantrill hoped to cap his career by assassinating President Lincoln; at least, he and his band hoped to reach Virginia and the environs of the national capital. But the guerilla leader's death cut short that later expedition, and the war ended soon afterward.

CHAPTER FIVE

George Caleb Bingham

IN GEORGE CALEB BINGHAM, Kansas City for twenty-five years, including the Civil War and reconstruction periods, had as one of its residents the principal artist of the early West. Like Kit Carson, Bingham was an adopted son of the frontier town of Franklin. Some years after the head of the wagon trails had moved up the river, and at a time when Bingham had acquired wide reputation for paintings done in various towns along the Missouri, he also moved up the river and became permanently established at Kansas City.

In addition to being well known as one of the country's foremost artists, Bingham took a prominent part in politics. He held a number of legislative and executive posts in the state government, and he received painting commissions from the Missouri legislature. In 1860 he had received $3,500 from the legislature for paintings of Henry Clay and Andrew Jackson. He was especially interested in his portrait of Jackson. Some-

71

thing of the artist's personality can be gathered from his experiences and comments in relation to this painting.

The equestrian portrait, celebrating Jackson's victory over the British at New Orleans, showed General Jackson waving his hat and urging his troops from the back of a spirited steed. Bingham consequently became interested in studying horses, and found it an advantage that Kansas City was the head of the wagon trails. "The windows of my studio," he wrote, "command the main avenue leading from Kansas City towards New Mexico, through which thousands of horses, oxen and mules are almost daily passing, and I have thus had an opportunity for observing by which I have been able to make the Old Hero's charger as near perfection as possible."

The artist was more than enthusiastic about this painting. "My portrait of Jackson," he wrote, "will be pronounced by connoisseurs and the public immeasurably superior to any similar work in the United States." Of the horse, Bingham wrote: "The jockeys who attended our County Fair last week will admit that he would have taken the premium from any animal in the ring. . . . But however perfect in symmetry, attitude and muscular development the horse may be regarded, the spectator will perceive at a glance that the still nobler rider fully maintains his proper prominence."

The portrait of Jackson was placed in the Senate Chamber of the Missouri State Capitol at Jefferson City. The artist himself was soon in Jefferson City, as the state's Adjutant General. A distinguished visitor, General William Tecumseh Sherman, arrived to tour the Missouri Capitol, and Bingham joined the governor's party which was following Sherman around the building.

Tact might well have suggested that General Sherman be advised that the artist was in the party. That precaution was somehow overlooked. As he reached the painting of Jackson,

General Sherman rocked back on his heels and chuckled.

"What horse," demanded Sherman, "would ever get itself into *that* position?"

Bingham, who was short (about the size of Napoleon and with as much fire and dignity), eyed General Sherman up and down for a few moments.

"That," snapped the artist, "is Old Hickory, a great soldier and statesman, and he had as much to do with the position of the horse as the artist had. If the artist had been painting *you* on horseback, he would probably have placed you astride a gentle, duck-legged pony ambling quietly along a country lane."

George Caleb Bingham was born in Augusta County, Virginia, on a farm which included Weir Cave, where his maternal grandfather had a gristmill powered by the South River. Bingham recalled the revolving wheels of this gristmill as the first wonder upon which his eyes opened. So well built was the mill that when he visited the place sixty years later, the wheels were still turning, and they continued to turn until shortly before the artist's death.

Bingham began to draw at the age of four, and was given paints with which he decorated the walls of the farm buildings. When the artist was eight years old, his father caught the prevailing fever to go west. The family moved to Franklin, the most distant settlement town in Missouri, arriving in 1819, the year the first steamboats reached there. Kit Carson was then a boy of ten, and Bingham was a boy of eight, in this village of log cabins and a few hundred people.

The artist's father bought the Square and Compass tavern, set up a cigar-making business, acquired land and was elected a county judge (supervisor), but lived only four years after the move to Franklin. Bingham was brought up and instructed by his mother. At the age of twelve he could make excellent pencil copies of the engravings that circulated in those days, and at the age of eighteen he knew most of the devices familiar to professional artists.

At the age of nineteen he set out for St. Louis to obtain formal instruction in art. En route, he suffered a severe attack of measles, in which he lost all his hair. Thereafter throughout his life, he wore a wig, which gave him some bad moments. A story famous in Missouri concerned a night shortly after his marriage when a wedding banquet was given for him. While he was seated in the chair of honor, a button on a waitress' sleeve caught on his wig, and she moved half way around the table with his wig dangling from her sleeve. Bingham rose to the occasion, retrieved his wig, and merely commented that since his own hair would not stay on his head, it was hardly to be expected that artificial hair would do so.

By the time he was twenty-four he was well established as a portrait painter in the river towns. He frequently finished an oil portrait in one day, and once did twenty-five portraits in thirty days. Bingham portraits, for which he was paid $25 to $60 each, became almost as common as silverware among the heirlooms of Missouri families.

At Columbia, Missouri, he acquired a sponsor in one Major James S. Rollins, an able and thoughtful man who served in Congress and was politically one of the most influential men in the state. Bingham's letters to Major Rollins provide a good record of the artist's life, revealing thoughts he might not have expressed in public. He eventually attended a few months at the Pennsylvania Academy of Fine Arts, then painted portraits for four years in Washington, D.C. When Frémont and Carson rose to prominence in the West, and the attention of the nation was on that part of the country, Bingham returned to Missouri and became famous for his Missouri scenes,— among them *Jolly Flatboatmen, Raftsmen Playing Cards* and *Fur Traders Descending the Missouri.*

Because of his strong views and fiery disposition, he became deeply involved in politics, despite frequent attempts to extricate himself. In 1846 he was elected to the state legislature by a margin of only seven votes. Being a member of a Whig minority, he was unseated in an election contest by an opponent named E. D. Sappington. After the contest, Bingham wrote: "If when you see me again you should not find me that pattern of purity which you have hitherto taken me to be, let the fact that I have been for the last four months full waist deep in Locofocoism plead something in my behalf. An angel could scarcely pass through what I have experienced without being contaminated. God help poor human nature. As soon as I get through with this experience and its consequences, I intend to strip off my clothes and bury them, scour my body all over with sand and water, put on a clean suit and keep out of the mire of politics *forever.*" However, he was soon writing, "I think we will either conquer in the next campaign or split our breeches"; and he was in fact returned to the legislature by a safe margin at the next election.

Much as he might profess to dislike politics, it was politics that inspired Bingham's masterpieces—*County Election, Stump Speaking* and *Verdict of the People.* He was in the habit of carrying a pad with him wherever he went. When he saw a face or figure which interested him, whether on the streets or elsewhere, he stopped and made a rapid sketch. In this way he acquired material for these best-known of his paintings, each of which contains from fifty to sixty highly individual figures, which he put in with a delicately pointed brush of stiffened sable hair. The effect is not unlike that of certain old Flemish paintings.

Of *Stump Speaking,* Bingham wrote: "In my orator I have endeavored to personify a wiry politician grown gray in the pursuit of office and service of party. His influence on the crowd is quite manifest, but I have placed behind him a shrewd, clear-headed opponent who is busy taking notes and who will, when the time comes, make sophisms fly like cobwebs from the housekeeper's broom." When the painting was exhibited, everyone said the orator was none other than E. D. Sappington, the man who had defeated Bingham in the election contest, and that the "shrewd, clear-headed opponent" was George Caleb Bingham himself. Moreover, also in the painting, with a bulldoglike, possessive eye fixed on the speaker, was a man easily recognized as a politically powerful former governor, M. M. Marmaduke. Marmaduke, first of two Missouri governors of this name, with difficulty was dissuaded from challenging the artist to a duel.

These pictures developed as he worked on them. When he was painting *County Election,* he wrote: "The gathering of the sovereigns is much larger than I had counted upon. A new head is continually popping up and demanding a place in the crowd, and as I am a thorough democrat it gives me pleasure to accommodate them all. The consequence of this impertinence on one side and indulgence on the other is that, instead of the select company which my plan first embraced, I have an audience which would be no discredit to the most populous precinct of Buncombe."

In another large group picture which he planned but did not find time to paint, Bingham intended to picture Senator Benton "Appealing to the People of Missouri." "That passage in which he designates the friends he has come to address as those who have 'heads to perceive and hearts to feel' the truth would afford, I think, the best point for pictorial representation. The action (gesture) which accompanied it and gave it such emphasis would display his fine portly figure to the best advantage and also tell with most happy effect on the faces of his audience." Elsewhere Bingham referred to "that contrast and variety of expression which confers the chief merit on such pictures," and to his purpose in "assuring that our social and political characteristics as daily and annually exhibited will not be lost for want of an art record rendering them full justice." In his pictures he did not fail to include the small boys and hound-dogs, and the voters who had drunk too deep of white mule.

Bingham's election series was completed, or ended, just before the opening of the Kansas Territory and the subsequent rush of events which made his earlier life seem pastoral by comparison. He had first moved to Independence, and then had established himself in Kansas City, from where he watched the approach of the Civil War. In 1854 he joined with Senator Benton in vigorously opposing the Kansas-Nebraska bill, or "Squatters' Sovereignty" bill, sponsored by Stephen A. Douglas—the measure which, by repealing the Missouri Compromise, reopened the slavery issue. During a visit in Washington, Bingham wrote:

Douglas' infamous bill will cause the partially smothered fires to break out with greater violence than ever. Such is the peculiar state of the parties at Washington that there is reason to fear it will pass. The opposition to it, however, is evidently greater than its unscrupulous author anticipated, and knowing that his political fortunes are staked upon it, he blows, bellows and leaps like 'the little black bull that came down from the mountains.' If, as Benton predicts, he should break his own neck in some of his gambols the service thereby rendered the country will be the only one which can place him upon the list of its benefactors.

When Senator Atchison was leading his motley armies of Missourians into Kansas, to beleaguer Lawrence and harass the Free State settlers, Bingham wrote that "Atchison, and all his stripe, whether Whigs or Democrats, must soon go to that limbo from which there is no reprieve. . . . Those who are most deeply interested in slavery will soon see the propriety of justice and moderation, such as will *conciliate* rather than exasperate neighbors, who will not be disposed (unless the Atchison outrages continue) to interfere with slavery upon our borders."

As the "Atchison outrages" continued, Bingham made one of his periodic attempts to escape into the world of art. He went to Düsseldorf, Germany, where he imagined that an artist "who sincerely worships truth and nature" could do his work in peace. Once in Düsseldorf, however, he watched all the hotel registers for American visitors, regaling them by the hour with his stories and taking the keenest interest in anything he could learn about the States.

Benton at this time was the old lion of Missouri politics. He was wounded and beset, but he was not dismayed. Five years after his defeat for the Senate, he still had the power to prevent the re-election of Senator Atchison. In fact, Benton so tied up the Missouri legislature in a three-way contest that it was unable to choose anyone, and Missouri for two years had only one senator. Then in his last bid, Benton made an unsuccessful campaign for governor; and though he was a Democrat and Bingham a Whig, he had the artist's whole-hearted support. "Old Bullion," wrote Bingham, "will once more be certain to make his power felt, if not in his own elevation at least in the downfall of his enemies. I regret that I cannot be on the ground to give him a vote."

On the Kansas issue, Bingham wrote: "Kansas, in spite of the stupendous rascality to secure it to slavery, will go, as it should go, for freedom. I trust Missouri will follow suit. Tell our friend Blair that I hope he will muster a strong party for emancipation by the time I get back, for as I shall be compelled to march to his music it will be a great comfort to feel my weakness braced by respectable numbers."

In December, 1860, after his return to Kansas City, Bingham wrote to his friend Major Rollins deploring the situation. He referred to "politics, that everlasting theme upon which, as a people, we become periodically stark mad. Such is preeminently our condition at the present time, and unless reason shall speedily resume her sway, I agree with you, that all the combined efforts of those who retain their sanity will not be sufficient to prevent us from going to the Devil." A Boone County political convention had evidently taken some action which looked toward secession, and on this subject Bingham added: "I cannot think the finale of your County meeting was at all creditable to old Boone. She is either somewhat affected by the prevailing disorder in the Upper Story, or looking to the speedy clearing up of the present storm she deems it wise to preserve her mule-raising condition by keeping on hand a few thoroughbred Jackasses."

But when the Kansas raiders were burning and pillaging in Missouri, Bingham turned sharply on them. His particular target, Colonel Jennison, on one occasion had herded all the male citizens of Independence into the town square, while his men systematically robbed the houses and stores. Jennison also made himself obnoxious by parading his troops unnecessarily through the streets of Independence and Kansas City, and by issuing fancy proclamations directed against the

Southern element. "He has far excelled the most renowned of our military heroes in the number and warlike tone of his proclamations," complained Bingham. "In the first of them he denounced the entire population of Jackson County as rebels, traitors and spies."

A sore point with the Missourians was that, whereas Quantrill and his guerillas were admitted outlaws, the Kansas raiders, Lane and Jennison, had official status in the Union Army. Jennison was a full colonel, in command of a so-called self-sustaining Kansas regiment. Regarding Jennison's elevation to the rank of colonel, Bingham, in 1862, struck a particularly mournful note.

> To those of us who never felt any neutrality in this contest, but have stood by our government in both word and deed since the first arm was raised against its authority, the apparent sanction which his conduct has received, *in high official quarters,* has been a source of the most profound humiliation. Gathered together in our little Fort, last summer, in defense of principles which inspired us with manly and patriotic pride, we could bear up, feeble as our numbers were, against even the disastrous intelligence from Bull Run, and bid defiance to the exulting traitors by whom we were surrounded. But when we beheld our glorious banner, endeared to us by cherished associations of the past, and held sacred and emblematical of all that was honorable, gallant and true, waving by authority over a regiment of *thieves, murderers* and *house burners,* led by an *outlaw,* whose only proper elevation would have been the *gallows,* we felt that we had received a blow from a doubly treacherous source, which, like the dagger of Brutus, inclined us to wrap our mantles about us and lie down in everlasting forgetfulness.

Then General Ewing's Order No. 11 further aroused the artist. Of Ewing, Bingham wrote: "He certainly excels in meanness all his Kansas predecessors"; and of Order No. 11, he declared: "It is well known that men were shot down in the very act of obeying the order." General Ewing, concerning Bingham, replied that the artist had so little understanding of the necessities of war that before he would commandeer a mule cart on a highway he would have to consult the Constitution to see if he had enough authority. But the artist had the last word. Some years after the war, General Ewing ran for governor of Ohio. His opponents circulated reproductions of Bingham's painting *Order No. 11*, with a legend about the cruelties under this order, and the painting was credited with playing an important part in Ewing's defeat.

In the post–Civil War period, the cattle trade at Kansas City greatly expanded. The town was frequented by gunmen who had kept their firearms when the fighting stopped, and gambling became an activity second only to the cattle industry. Bingham had invested in Kansas City real estate, and found the developments not to his liking. In 1874 he wrote: "The numerous gambling holes and kindred establishments, by driving proper business to other quarters, have so reduced my rents that I have been compelled to paint portraits this winter for the support of my family."

As a result of the gambling, he was induced to accept a post as a Kansas City police commissioner. He was by this time always addressed as "General Bingham." Preserving his military bearing, though his wig was frequently awry, he personally led raids in which two or three hundred gamblers were turned into the streets. He later wrote with some surprise that he found he still had friends among the gamblers. The reform, which lasted several months, was Bingham's last dramatic appearance on the Kansas City scene. During his life there, he was highly respected both for his art and his political opinions, yet many stories make clear that his contemporaries did not miss the comical effect produced by the combination of his extreme vigor, his dignity, his wig, and his bantam size. His letters indicate that he also appreciated this effect, and enjoyed the license it gave him to indulge his taste for colorful action and speech.

The painting, *Order No. 11,* was a major preoccupation for the artist in his last years. It became so famous, and so controversial, that he was continually engaged in defending it. He contended that it did not reflect upon the Union troops in general, but only upon the "Kansas Red Legs and their equally demoniac associates." His last statement on the subject was printed after his death, under the heading, "A Voice from the Tomb." During the course of this and other controversies, Bingham's sympathies had been drawn more and more to the Southern side, where in fact his nativity lay; and, although he had been a strong Union man, he left part of his estate to a home for Confederate veterans at Higginsville, Missouri.

CHAPTER SIX

The Crime of a Century

THE CIVIL WAR had been over for more than four years, according to the official way of figuring, but a good many of its effects still lingered in Missouri. It was December 7, 1869, a cloudy and fairly cold day. Two or three inches of snow lay on the ground, the house doors were closed and the fires were burning in the stoves. Near noon the town of Gallatin, in Daviess County, Missouri, three counties northeast of Kansas City, was waiting as towns do for something in the way of business or excitement to come along, when two young men, mounted on spirited horses, rode up to the Daviess County Savings Bank. One of the men dismounted and, handing his bridle rein to the other, quickly entered the bank.

A man named McDowell was in the bank on routine business, and the cashier, John W. Sheets, was behind the counter. The booted stranger presented a $100 bill and asked the cashier to change it. Sheets took the bill, walked back to the safe, took out a handful of bills and returned to the counter.

He was in the act of counting out the change when the stranger, without speaking a word, thrust forward a large revolver and shot the cashier through the heart. Almost immediately he fired a second shot which went through the cashier's brain. The stranger then turned the gun toward McDowell, backed around the bank railing and, keeping McDowell covered, proceeded with one hand to gather up all the cash he could find in the safe and till, and to stuff it into his pocket. He obtained about seven hundred dollars.

These details concerning the Gallatin bank robbery appeared in the newspapers of the day, together with additional details of the robbers' escape. As soon as they heard the shooting, eight or ten Gallatin citizens snatched up weapons and began moving down the street toward the bank. The "murderous scoundrel" in the bank, said the papers, then heard a sharp cry of warning from his companion outside, and rushed into the street. In two bounds he would have been astride his horse, except that the horse, frightened by the shouts and the shooting, made a plunge just as the murderer, with one foot in the stirrup, made a spring to mount. The suddenness of the horse's movement threw the robber to the ground and he was dragged head downward for thirty or forty feet, with one foot caught in the stirrup. Finally he succeeded in disengaging himself, but for several moments he lay on the ground as though stunned. His horse—the most important clew left behind—cantered off down the street and turned up a side road.

The armed citizens by this time had drawn a little closer, and were firing steadily at the fallen robber. In spite of the bullets, his mounted companion rode back and, swinging low in the saddle, helped him up behind. The two robbers, mounted double, then galloped out of town.

Within a few minutes, fifteen or twenty citizens had

saddled horses and set off in pursuit. They had high hopes of catching the robbers because both were on one overloaded horse. However, about a mile out of town the robbers encountered a farmer named Daniel Smoot. Smoot was riding a good horse, which they took; and now properly mounted they had no difficulty in eluding pursuit.

Between Gallatin and the town of Kidder, Missouri, they talked to several persons, and told at least two of them that they had robbed the bank at Gallatin and had shot the cashier. On nearing Kidder they fell in with a Methodist minister, the Reverend Mr. Helm, and forced him to guide them around the town. The younger of the robbers told the Reverend Mr. Helm that he was a brother of Bloody Bill Anderson, the noted guerilla. He said he was the one who entered the bank, and that he had killed S. P. Cox "if he had not made a mistake in his man." He claimed he had done this in order to avenge his brother Bill's death.

It was true that Bloody Bill Anderson's career had been ended by a bullet from the gun of Lieutenant S. P. Cox of the Union Army. The murdered cashier, John W. Sheets, had served as a captain in the Union Army and bore enough resemblance to Lieutenant Cox so that he might, conceivably, have been mistaken for him. It was also true that Bloody Bill Anderson had a brother who might have entertained some ideas of revenge. But it was exceedingly improbable that Bloody Bill's brother, if he had exacted revenge, would so identify himself while still in the midst of flight. It seemed much more likely that the story of revenge had been thought up to divert suspicion by someone familiar with Bloody Bill's family affairs and the manner of his death, probably by a former member of Anderson's guerilla band. The latter description fitted Jesse W. James, upon whom suspicion soon fell.

Horses were easily identified. People were accustomed to noting their markings and gait, and careful records were kept of the ownership of each horse. And, as the Kansas City *Times* reported on December 16, 1869, the horse which had been left behind at Gallatin was identified as belonging to "a young man named James, whose mother and step-father live about four miles from Centreville, Clay County, near the Cameron branch of the Hannibal & St. Joe railroad"—in other words, a short ride north of Kansas City. The city was on the south bank of the Missouri River, in Jackson County, while the north bank of the river was Clay County.

The Gallatin robbery was the sixth to occur at intervals of five or six months after the close of the Civil War. It was known that these bank robberies were being carried out by the former Missouri guerillas, usually in bands of six or seven, since in several instances they had given the rebel yell and had otherwise identified themselves. But the Gallatin robbery was the first with which the name of James was connected, and was also the first in which a tangible clew had been left behind. When in addition the citizens of Gallatin learned that both Jesse James and his brother Frank were former guerillas, "experienced in horse and revolver work," as the newspapers said; and that these two brothers operated as a pair, they had no doubt that Jesse James, the younger and more trigger nervous of the two, was the man who had entered the bank and shot the cashier, and that Frank James, a cool man under difficulties, was the one who rode back under fire and rescued him after he had been thrown in the street.

As soon as all this had been made clear, two determined and heavily armed Gallatin citizens rode off to Clay County in the first of many attempts, all equally unsuccessful, to capture the James boys.

The two Gallatin citizens stopped off at Liberty, the seat of Clay County, where the sheriff assigned Deputy John S. Thomason to accompany them in order to make the arrests. Thomason took along his son Oscar. That made four horsemen, two from Gallatin and two from Liberty, that set forth to arrest the bandits.

Frank and Jesse James were sons of a Baptist minister, a farmer-preacher who went to California during the gold rush. The father had died of fever in California, and their mother had married a Dr. Samuels, a country doctor who also farmed. The Samuels farm was about twenty miles from Liberty, a long ride which now gave the four pursuers an opportunity to discuss the Gallatin robbery and to lay down a strategy for the capture of the brothers if they resisted.

When still several miles from the Samuels farmhouse, the four left the road and followed a line of timber, which enabled them to emerge near the house without having been seen in advance. The two Gallatin citizens were posted at the edge of the timber in such a way that they could fire upon anyone emerging from either the front or the back of the house. The deputy, carrying a shotgun, and his son, with a drawn revolver, then approached the house, while the two men from Gallatin sat their horses with raised rifles trained on the front door.

The door was opened by a small colored boy, who took one look at the heavily armed visitors, then ran as fast as he could go toward the barn. The deputies thought at first that the boy had merely been frightened by the guns. But a few seconds after he reached the barn, the farthest door burst open and the James brothers, already mounted, sprang out to make a run for it. They were riding low after the fashion of the guerillas, and they jumped their horses at full gallop over the lot fence.

The Gallatin citizens fired without effect, while the deputy and his son ran for their horses. The four then started off in close pursuit. However, the horse of Deputy Thomason was the only one of the four that would take the lot fence. While the other three riders were dismounting and knocking the top rails from a section of the fence, Deputy Thomason rode on alone and was soon lost from view in the brush.

Exactly what happened next was in some dispute. Deputy Thomason said that in the course of several miles he fired a number of times with his revolver, but without effect. He then dismounted to try to get one good shot with a rifle. When he dismounted, his horse broke away and ran on, whereupon the James boys waited for it and shot the riderless animal in the head. The James boys, on the other hand, said they shot Thomason's horse for his own protection, and permitted him to escape through the brush.

In either case, the horse was killed. An hour or so after he had started, Deputy Thomason reappeared on foot at the Samuels farmhouse. He asked Mrs. Samuels to lend him a horse. Mrs. Samuels, naturally wrought up over the shooting, at first refused, and "gave him a piece of her mind."

The James brothers' mother was strong in defense of her own, and had many other good qualities, but she had a temper, and was sharp-tongued. It was freely reported in the neighborhood, and was even recounted in one of the Kansas City newspapers, that her first husband, the Reverend Robert James, went to California not so much to search for gold as to get away from his wife. But if this was true, it should be added that her second husband, the patient Dr. Samuels, always got along well with her, and her sons always came home regularly to see her, even under extremely hazardous conditions. Perhaps her hot temper was of short duration, as in this case. For after telling Deputy Thomason that if her sons had shot his horse, she was sure they had done so to keep from shooting him, and she was not sure they had made the right choice—after these and similar statements, she presently relented and agreed to lend him a horse. Deputy Thomason then was obliged to return to Liberty without his intended prisoners, although he was mounted on one of their horses.

The Kansas City *Times* in reporting Deputy Thomason's experience said, "Clay County is pretty thoroughly aroused, and parties are organizing to hunt up the brothers." If this was the case, nothing came of the hunt. A year and a half passed before the James boys again figured in the news. By this time they had joined forces with Cole Younger and his brothers, and two or three other former guerillas. There were seven bandits in all when on June 3, 1871, they rode north into Corydon, Iowa, and robbed the bank of $40,000. This was the biggest haul of their careers. On April 29, 1872, they robbed the bank at Columbia, Kentucky, of $200 and killed the cashier. On September 23, 1872, they put on masks, galloped up to the box office of the Kansas City Fair, and galloped off with the day's receipts, nearly $10,000. On May 21, 1873, they obtained $4,000 from the bank at St. Genevieve, Missouri, and near Adair, Iowa, on July 2, 1873, eight years after the Civil War, they carried out their first train robbery, getting about $3,000. A stagecoach robbery near Hot Springs, Arkansas, and a second train robbery at Gadshill, Missouri, followed early in 1874. By this time the names of the James and Younger boys were known throughout Missouri, and in fact throughout the land.

Immediately following the Civil War, in 1865, the "Drake Constitution" was adopted for Missouri. This measure, deeply resented, was in effect through two elections. It disfranchised the former Confederates, and prohibited their practicing professions, acting as deacons in a church, or engaging in various other activities. During the same period, a certain number of vengeful officeholders were active in harassing former Confederates, especially former guerillas. These officeholders brought old charges against them, some of the charges relating to acts committed during the war, and in other ways made it difficult for the Southerners to return to peaceful pursuits. On the other hand, a number of Missouri guerillas returned to Missouri farms and were never molested. The record does not show that the James boys were hunted or molested until the time of the Gallatin bank robbery, more than four years after the war. But many of the guerillas left for other states, in the belief that Missouri was an unsafe place for them.

Missourians looked on the James boys with mixed feelings. Missourians as well as people in other states suffered from the outlaws' operations, and if they had been caught by one of the posses that pursued them in the early days, they would probably have been hanged. But, since they repeatedly escaped, they came to symbolize the resentment which Missourians felt for the "law" which had been imposed during and after the war. There was a strong disposition to feel that they were not guilty of the crimes attributed to them; or that, if they were guilty, they had been driven by persecution into their desperate acts. It was certainly true that the James and Younger boys had been fine, upstanding youths before the war, and had become outlaws under abnormal circumstances. And it was not to be forgotten that they had been Southern fighting men, who had helped to protect the countryside from the Kansas raiders and to avenge the wrongs the raiders had committed.

Whatever its basis, the fact remained that the James boys and their fellow bandits always had more friends than the men who hunted them. This was especially true after 1874, when the hunt for them was placed in the hands of Pinkerton detectives, who, coming from Chicago, had the additional disadvantage of being outsiders in Missouri.

The Pinkertons established an agency in Kansas City, with a staff of ten men detailed to hunt down the James and Younger boys. The detectives disguised themselves as cattle buyers and farm hands, and hoped by this means to draw close enough to their quarry either to capture or to kill them. But the disguises were not effective, and within eight months three of the detectives had been killed.

Two of the slain detectives had ventured into St. Clair County, where the four Younger brothers had a great many relatives and were known to hide out. In their roles as cattle buyers, the detectives were making their way to the home of one of the Younger relatives, when they stopped at a farmhouse to ask directions. The residents of the farmhouse where they stopped were related to the Youngers, and two of the Younger brothers were then visiting at this very house. The Youngers did not think that the strangers looked like cattle buyers, so they followed them up the road. In the shooting that ensued, both of the detectives and John Younger, the youngest of the brothers, were killed.

The third detective disguised himself as a farm hand, and thought to obtain work in the James neighborhood. He walked out of a Kansas City hotel in his disguise, and as that hotel was not frequented by farm hands, he was easily spotted. Word of his coming long preceded him into the James neighborhood. The next night his body was found in the middle of a road just outside Independence. The body had been brought back across the river as a warning to other detectives to stay out of Clay County. His slayers were never identified.

A fourth detective was a little more successful. He spoke the dialect of the region, and apparently was familiar with its customs. Using the name of Jack Ladd, he obtained a job on the farm of Daniel Askew, near the James home. He had no idea of a single-handed attack upon the James brothers, but he attended church socials, became acquainted with Dr. and Mrs. Samuels, and gathered such information as he could. On January 21, 1875, he reported to the Pinkerton headquarters in Kansas City that the James boys were at the Samuels farmhouse, "to visit the old lady for a week or two."

Four nights later, on January 25, a party of five detectives, moving under cover of darkness, crept up on the Samuels farmhouse. One of the detectives carried a ball of cotton waste which had been soaked in kerosene, and another carried a bomb, also wrapped in kerosene-soaked cotton so that it gave the same appearance.

The Samuels farmhouse was a small one, painted white with green shutters. On the ground floor there was a large room which served both as kitchen and dining room. The detectives forced a window leading into the room, then struck a match to the ball of cotton waste and tossed it flaming through the window. A colored woman, who looked after the Samuels children, and one of the children were sleeping on a cot in the large room. Their cries immediately brought Dr. and Mrs. Samuels, aroused from their sleep and dressed in their nightclothes. On either side of a large fireplace were a number of tobacco sticks, used in holding tobacco for curing. Dr. and Mrs. Samuels each took one of these sticks and pushed the flaming ball of cotton waste into the fireplace.

Then a second burning missile came through the window.

"The second ball was not like the first, but looked like it," Dr. Samuels said later. "Thinking it to be another fireball, my wife at first tried to push it into the hearth, but finding it much heavier said, 'Doctor, try and see if you can get it to the hearth.' I still had a stick in my hand, but found it too light to move the shell. I then got a shovel and began to push it toward the hearth, and just as I succeeded, the shell exploded. It seemed to me the room grew black as night. I was blown against the ceiling and the room was pitch black. Outside I heard several 'hurrahs'; then the groan of my little boy and the agonized cries of my wife, who told me her right arm was blown to pieces. The detectives began cross-firing past the house, then left, one man calling 'Hurry up, boys, for we'll have to come back again just to keep up appearances.' As soon as they left I went to the door and called for help, and at last some of the neighbors came."

The bomb-throwing by the Pinkerton detectives exhibited a disregard for women and children that even Quantrill, in war, would not have tolerated. It became known in Missouri, and in the newspapers of the country, as "the crime of the century." The detectives did not reappear in the neighborhood, either that night or ever again. Although Dr. Samuels had been closest to the bomb and had been blown against the ceiling, he was only bruised. But his wife's right arm had to be amputated above the elbow, and their eight-year-old boy, Archie Samuels, half brother of the James boys, died at dawn from a wound in his side caused by a fragment of the bomb. Whether the James boys were at home when the bomb was thrown was never known; if they were, they were probably sleeping near their horses in the barn.

Following the bombing, there was much sentiment in favor of granting an amnesty which would enable the bandits to surrender and return to peaceful occupations without fear of penalty. Representative Jefferson Jones, from the rock-ribbed Democracy of Callaway County, known to his friends as "General Jeff" and long a figure in Missouri politics, agreed to lead the amnesty movement in the Missouri legislature. He prepared a long resolution which stated that the James and Younger boys were being "driven from the fields of honest industry," and which referred to the Pinkerton detectives as "foreign mercenaries, armed with the power to capture or kill them." The resolution also expressed the opinion that "most, if not all the offenses with which they are charged have been committed by others, perhaps by those pretending to hunt them."

The resolution was something of an embarrassment to the Democratic party in Missouri. On the one hand the James and Younger boys had fought for the South, they were patriots of a lost cause, and they were entitled to consideration from others who had been on the same side. But the bank and train robberies attributed to them could not be lightly dismissed, since they were causing Missouri to be known as "the robber state," and the phrase "poor old Missouri" had come into common use because of the state's inability to catch the outlaws. Moreover, granting a pardon to men who refused to surrender and could not be caught, and consequently had never been convicted of anything, was a procedure unknown to statecraft. So in the end the resolution merely provided that the governor should issue a proclamation lifting the ban of outlawry against the bandits, and promising them a fair trial if they surrendered.

This resolution might have brought the bandits in, but was never finally adopted by the legislature. The first time the resolution came before the House of Representatives it was favored by a vote of fifty-eight to thirty-nine, just short of the two-thirds majority required. The St. Louis *Democrat* said it would certainly pass on reconsideration, since only seven votes were needed and thirty-two members were absent. Then a new incident occurred: The farmer, Daniel Askew, who unknowingly had given employment to the Pinkerton agent before the bombing, was shot and killed by three riflemen who hid behind his woodpile and fired when he stepped out on the porch. The general belief was that the James boys had nothing to do with this shooting, and that the murder of Askew was the work of some of their over-zealous partisans. Nevertheless, the slaying of Askew was another act of violence which made the Jones resolution even more embarrassing. Consequently, the resolution languished and was never reconsidered.

In the months following the failure of the amnesty movement, the third and fourth train robberies and another bank robbery or two were committed by the James-Younger boys. The next year, in September, 1876, an attempted raid on the bank at Northfield, Minnesota, led to the break-up of the original bandit outfit.

For the Northfield raid there were eight bandits. Three of them entered the bank, while the other five rode up and down outside, clearing the street. Their plans at Northfield went badly awry when the cashier refused to open the safe, made a dive for his gun, but was finally shot and killed. A number of Northfield citizens armed themselves in short order, and began firing from windows and doorways on the bandits outside. Two of the bandits were killed and left dead in the street, and the six who managed to get out of town were all more or less severely wounded. One of the Youngers was so badly wounded that another had to mount double with him to hold him on the horse, and the retreat of the bandits was so slow that their pursuers were able to surround them.

The three Younger brothers were captured, and a companion was killed—the third bandit to be killed. That left only the James boys still at large, with more than a thousand well-armed Minnesotans on the hunt for them. In spite of everything, the James brothers got away, and the retreat from Northfield became one of the most celebrated incidents of their career. They were surrounded in a woods and broke through the picket line at night. The pickets turned a heavy fire on them, killing their horses, but the brothers disappeared in a cornfield. They found a barn and stole two horses in the dark. Riding bareback, they put a great deal of distance behind them before dawn. The next day a farmer reported that he was forced to trade horses with them, and that the bandits were so stiff they had to climb a fence to mount. Reports concerning them continued all across Minnesota. They stopped and forced a physician to dress their wounds, and they fought a gun battle with a posse that located them. They apparently reached the Missouri River near Sioux City, Iowa. Traveling in a rowboat by night, and hiding in the brush by day, they made their way down the river until they reached their native Clay County.

Up to the time of the Northfield raid, a total of fourteen bank robberies and four train robberies had been attributed either to the James or the Younger boys, or to both. Yet thousands in Missouri had refused to believe that these men so often accused were guilty. Their skepticism had been given support in 1875 when a train robbery at Muncie, Kansas, and two bank robberies, one at Corinth, Mississippi, and another in Tennessee, had occurred on the same day. Too-hasty correspondents in each town had attributed all three robberies to the James and Younger boys. Even the Gallatin

John Brown

bank robbery was regarded by many as a trumped-up affair, since Frank and Jesse James, as was their custom, published lengthy statements in the Kansas City papers declaring themselves innocent. A feature of their long outlawry was that, although they could not be caught, they could always be reached by the insertion of a notice in one of the papers. No photographs of either were in circulation, and under assumed names Jesse James was able to live for periods of several months in Kansas City. It was said that he sometimes played cards of an evening with a member of the police force, and that he once was forced to beg off when asked to join a posse in his own pursuit.

After the Northfield holdup, the idea that the James boys were innocent could no longer be entertained. Several months earlier a man named Hobbs Kerry had been captured in one of the train robberies and had named the members of the outlaw band, listing the James and Younger brothers, Clell Miller, Charlie Pitts, and Bill Chadwell. The last three, Miller, Pitts, and Chadwell, were the bandits killed at Northfield. The Younger brothers had been captured and locked in a Minnesota prison. So the Kerry confession had to be accepted, and with it the fact that Frank and Jesse James undoubtedly were the two who escaped at Northfield. Even so, many in Missouri did not find it possible to take sides against them. While the bandits were in the midst of their retreat from Northfield, sheriffs along the route reported receiving from the Missouri border well-composed letters which, instead of urging them in the usual way to do their duty and catch the fleeing outlaws, presented reasons why they should not. "The singular fidelity of the citizens of Kansas City and Independence to the James boys has never been understood," said an editorial of the time. "But it should be remembered that in the cruel border warfare from 1860 to 1864 the guerillas zealously defended the people of Jackson County from the tyranny and oppression of the unbridled Federal forces that made frequent raids from Kansas for the purpose of plunder and murder. . . . It was a debt of gratitude."

CHAPTER SEVEN

He Came In

THE NORTHFIELD BANK RAID was followed by three years of quiet, during which Frank and Jesse James were said to have settled down under assumed names on farms in Arkansas. Both of the outlaws had married neighborhood girls. Jesse James's bride was his first cousin, blonde Zerelda Mimms, who had been something of a belle in Kansas City. They were married in 1874, after the Gadshill train robbery, in a festive ceremony. Jesse James threw aside his usual caution to ride down the main street of his home town of Kearney—with a rifle, however, across his saddle horn—to receive the congratulations of the townspeople.

By the time of the Northfield raid and the move to Arkansas, Jesse James had two children and Frank James had one. Although the brothers were always heavily armed, they were able, in the still somewhat disordered times, to pass as peaceable family men during the three years they spent in Arkansas.

In 1879 Jesse James led a return to Missouri. In the next three years he carried out three train robberies, all within convenient horseback distance of his old Clay County home. Twice ties were placed on the track to stop Chicago & Alton trains, after which the bandits robbed the passengers and rifled the express cars; and a Rock Island train was robbed in similar fashion. The country's railroad systems were thrown into a state of agitation. After two or three bullets had found their mark, passengers began refusing to travel across Missouri. Probably because conditions had grown more settled and peaceful, these last train robberies had much greater impact on the public mind than the earlier ones, and Jesse James became a national legend.

Whether Frank James took part in these last train robberies was in dispute. A jury held he did not. In any case, Jesse James seemed to be in command, and the restraining influence of the older brother seemed to be absent. The younger James carried a well-marked Bible in his pocket, did not drink or smoke, and had a pleasant smile and a boyish habit of blinking his eyes rapidly; but shooting people rested lightly on his conscience. And the shooting raised a public clamor that the James boys be put down.

Jesse James faced another difficulty by this time. Fifteen years had now passed since the Civil War, and young men he could get for his rejuvenated band had passed through no such initiation in guerilla warfare as had his early companions. They were not outlaws for the same reasons now, and they lacked the skill and fortitude of those with whom he had ridden before. One of them, Robert Ford, soon betrayed him for the reward offered by Governor Thomas T. Crittenden of Missouri. Three or four others would have betrayed him, if they had found the opportunity.

Thomas T. Crittenden, the man who stopped the James

boys, became governor of Missouri in January, 1881. Soon afterward occurred the Winston train robbery, in which the conductor and a stonemason, who was a passenger, were killed. The governor determined to offer a large reward for the outlaws. Being prevented by the state constitution from offering a reward of more than $300 for a person, he induced the railroads to make up a reward purse of $50,000. Five thousand dollars was offered for the capture of any member of the James band and an additional $5,000 was posted for the conviction of either Frank or Jesse James—making a total of $10,000 each on the heads of Frank and Jesse.

Within a few months three members of the James band had signified to the authorities their desire to collect the rewards. One of these, a bandit named Dick Liddil, surrendered and placed himself under protection for the purpose of acting as a witness against either of the James boys. Then twenty-year-old Robert Ford and his older brother Charles, sent their sister, a lady of low repute, to the governor to say that they were ready to bring down Jesse James himself.

In view of the controversy that followed, it is well to note exactly what the governor did. In the first place, he offered a large reward, furnished not by the state but by the railroads. In the second place, he talked to the Fords' sister, the lady of low repute, and then to Robert Ford about the furtherance of the project. Governor Crittenden always stressed that in his proclamation of the rewards he did not say "dead or alive," and in fact indicated a preference for capture by offering an additional reward for conviction. But Robert Ford testified at the Jesse James inquest that the governor in conversation said "dead or alive," and certainly the Fords never had any hope of bringing in Jesse alive.

What happened to Jesse James on a warm April day in 1882 is best told by an unremembered newspaper reporter who telegraphed the first story from St. Joseph, Missouri, and who wrote with a true feeling for great events. His account began:

St. Joseph, Mo., April 3—Between eight and nine o'clock this morning, Jesse James, the Missouri outlaw, before whose acts the deeds of Fra Diavolo and Dick Turpin dwindle into insignificance, was killed by a boy twenty years old, named Robert Ford, at his temporary residence at Thirteenth and Lafayette Streets, in this city. In the light of all moral reasoning the shooting was wholly unjustifiable, but the law was vindicated. The large reward offered by the state for the body of the brigand doubtless will go to the man who had the courage to draw a revolver on the outlaw when his back was turned, as in this case.

There followed details of how Jesse James had come to St. Joseph from Kansas City six months before, traveling under the name of Howard and bringing his wife and two children in a wagon. He had rented a small house, and was planning, from the St. Joseph vantage point, to look over the banks in northern Kansas. More immediately, he had planned to go that evening for a raid on the bank at Platte City, Missouri. He had with him the brothers Robert and Charles Ford, who had no idea of trying to capture him, considering the attempt suicidal, but who for months had been looking for a suitable opportunity to kill him. The St. Joseph story continued:

The opportunity they had wished for came this morning. Breakfast was over. Charles Ford and Jesse James had been in the stable currying their horses, preparatory for their night ride. On returning to the room where Robert was, Jesse said: "It's an awfully hot day." He pulled off his coat and vest and tossed them on the bed. Then he said: "I guess I'll take off my pistols for fear

someone will see them if I walk in the yard." He un-
buckled the belt in which he carried two .45 caliber
revolvers, one a Smith & Wesson and the other a Colt,
and laid them on the bed with his coat and vest. He then
picked up a dusting brush with the intention of dusting
some pictures that were hung on the wall. To do this he
got on a chair.

His back was now turned to the brothers, who silently
stepped between Jesse and his revolvers, and, at a motion
from Charley they both drew their guns. Robert was the
quickest of the two. In one instant he had the long
weapon to a level with his eye with the muzzle no more
than four feet from the back of the outlaw's head. Even
in that motion, quick as thought, there was something
that did not escape the acute ears of the hunted man. He
made a motion as if to turn his head to ascertain the cause
of that suspicious sound. But too late. A nervous pressure
of the trigger, a quick flash, sharp report and the well-
directed ball crashed through the outlaw's skull.

There was no outcry, just a swaying of the body, and it
fell heavily back upon the carpet. The shot had been
fatal, and all the bullets in the chamber of Charley's
revolver still directed at Jesse's head could not more
effectually have decided the fate of the greatest bandit
and free-booter that ever figured on the pages of the
country's history. The ball had entered the base of the
skull and made its way out through the forehead, over
the left eye. It had been fired from a Colt's .45, improved
pattern, silver-mounted and pearl-handled gun, presented by the dead man to his slayer only a few days ago.

Mrs. James was in the kitchen when the shooting was
done, divided from the room in which the bloody
tragedy occurred by a dining room. She heard the shot,
and dropping her household duties ran into the front
room. She saw her husband lying on his back, and his
slayers each holding a revolver in hand, making for the
fence in the rear of the house. Robert had reached the
enclosure and was in the act of scaling it when she
stepped to the door and called to him, "Robert, you have

done this; come back." Robert answered, "I swear to God I did not." They then returned to where she stood. Mrs. James ran to the side of her husband and lifted up his head. Life was not extinct, and, when asked if he was hurt, it seemed to her that he wanted to say something, and couldn't. She tried to wash away the blood that was coursing over his face from the hole in his forehead, but it seemed to her that the blood would come faster than she could wash it away, and in her hands Jesse died. Charley Ford explained to Mrs. James that "a pistol had accidentally gone off." "Yes," said Mrs. James, "I guess it went off on purpose"; and the Ford brothers left the house.

The death of Jesse James caused a great stir, and much comment in the newspapers of the country. The New York *Sun* said that bad as Jesse might have been, he was a better man than his slayer Robert Ford, and "To make a new murderer in the process of getting rid of an old one is a practice that cannot be justified." The Cincinnati *Star-Times* said, "If Governor Crittenden of Missouri reads the newspapers extensively, he has discovered that public opinion severely condemns assassination by law, even in the case of a notorious desperado and outlaw. Not a single reputable paper in the land justifies the part he plays in the conspiracy to murder James." Another comment was: "If Thomas H. Benton in the days of his glory had been assassinated, the murderer could not have been more vengefully abused than Governor Crittenden has been abused for the death of Jesse James."

Many newspapers tempered their accounts, saying that while they did not excuse Ford or the governor, yet the death of the outlaw was necessary. These papers recalled that Jesse James had not given his victims a sporting chance to defend themselves, and estimated that in the course of his career he had shed enough innocent blood to swim in. But the editorial which became much the most famous on the Missouri border was written by a man who was in no mood for temporizing. It came from the pen of Major John N. Edwards, a former editor of the Kansas City *Times* who at this time was editing his own paper in the town of Sedalia, Missouri.

Major John N. Edwards was a great admirer of all the former guerillas, and other Southern fighting men. He could account for the fact that the North had won the war only by supposing that "in the same proportions sheep would have trampled lions to death," an analogy which he considered very apt. He had always been friendly with the James boys. Some said that on the day the James boys galloped up to the box office of the Kansas City Fair and galloped off with nearly $10,000, they galloped back the same night to present Major Edwards with a $500 Jergerson repeater watch. Whether that was true or not, Major Edwards wrote in sorrow as well as indignation of the day of Jesse's death. He began his editorial calmly with a quotation:

> *Let not Caesar's servile minions*
> *Mock the lion thus laid low . . .*

He then warmed to his subject.

No one among all the hired cowards, hard on the hunt for blood money, dared face this wonderful outlaw, one even against twenty, until he had disarmed himself and turned his back to his assassins—the first and only time in a career which has passed from the realm of almost fabulous romance into that of history.

We called him outlaw, and he was, but Fate made him so. When the war came he was just turned fifteen. The border was all aflame with steel, and fire, and ambuscade, and slaughter. He flung himself into a band which had a black flag for a banner and devils for riders. What he did he did, and it was fearful. But it was war. It was Missouri against Kansas. It was Jim Lane and Jennison against Quantrill, Anderson and Todd.

When the war closed Jesse James had no home. Proscribed, hunted, shot, driven away from his people, a price put on his head—what else could the man do, with such a nature, except what he did do? He had to live. It was his country. The graves of his kindred were there. He refused to be banished from his birthright, and when he was hunted he turned savagely about and hunted his hunters. Would to God he were alive today to make a righteous butchery of a few more of them!

One call would have brought five hundred men to surround his house and capture Jesse, Major Edwards said; but he had been killed by treachery so that a few men, the Ford brothers and two or three officers, could get all of the reward. "It was his blood the bloody wretches were after—blood which would bring money in the official market of Missouri." The major also seemed to be thinking a good deal of the Ford brothers' sister, the lady of low repute, and of the fact that the witness Dick Liddil's common-law wife had figured in the negotiations. His editorial continued:

And this great commonwealth leagued with a lot of self-confessed robbers, highwaymen and prostitutes to have one of its citizens assassinated before it was positively known that he had ever committed a single crime worthy of death.

Of course everything that can be said about the dead man to justify the manner of his killing will be said; but who is saying it? Those with the blood of Jesse James on their guilty souls. Those who conspired to murder him. Those who wanted the reward, and would invent any lie or concoct any diabolical story to get it. They have succeeded, but such a cry of horror and indignation at the infernal deed is even now thundering over the land that if a single one of the miserable assassins had either manhood, conscience or courage, he would go, as another Judas, and hang himself.

If Jesse James had been hunted down as any other criminal and killed while trying to escape or resisting arrest, not a word would have been said to the contrary. He had sinned and he had suffered. In his death the majesty of the law would have been vindicated; but here the law itself becomes a murderer. It leagues with murderers. It borrows money to pay and reward murderers. It promises immunity and protection to murderers. It is itself a murderer—the most abject, the most infamous, and the most cowardly ever known to history.

The hand that slew him had to be a traitor's! Into all the warp and woof of the devil's work there were threads woven by the fingers of a harlot. What a spectacle! Missouri, with splendid companies and regiments of militia. Missouri, with 117 sheriffs, as brave and efficient on the average as any men on earth. Missouri, with a watchful and vigilant marshal in every one of her principal towns and cities. Missouri, with every screw and cog and crank and lever and wheel of her administrative machinery in perfect working order. Missouri, with all her order, progress and development, had yet to surrender all these in the face of a single man—a hunted, lied upon, proscribed and outlawed man—and ally with some five or six cutthroats and prostitutes that the majesty of the law might be vindicated, and the good name of the state saved from all further reproach!

Saved? Why, the whole state reeks today with a double orgy—that of lust and that of murder. What the men failed to do the women accomplished.

Tear the two bears from the flag of Missouri! Put thereon, in place of them, as more appropriate, a thief blowing out the brains of an unarmed victim, and a brazen harlot, naked to the waist and spattered to the brows with blood!

Thus Major Edwards concluded his editorial, and there was no doubt that he spoke the sentiments of a good many people. Governor Crittenden was placed in a difficult political position, and the railroads which had contributed the $50,000 for the rewards began to regret their act. Both the governor and the railroad managers were in a conciliatory mood toward what might be called the James boys' public. Bending before the storm of public indignation, the railroads joined in a plan to enable Frank James to surrender quietly on terms as favorable to him as possible, with Major Edwards acting as go-between.

A purse of $5,000 was raised in Frank James's behalf. Most of the money was contributed by railroads "from considerations of policy," the newspapers said. The money was needed to pay lawyers and to meet other expenses in connection with quashing and quieting charges against him in other states, thereby preventing extradition. Governor Crittenden was disposed to agree that Frank James should not be taken to any other state. But the governor was a stickler for law, and he insisted that the usual procedures within the state must be carried out. Mrs. Samuels, now one-armed, went to Jefferson City and had what the newspapers described as "an old-fashioned row" with the governor because he would not absolutely promise to grant Frank James a pardon if he should be convicted of a crime. Despite her failure to extract a promise, Governor Crittenden's favorable disposition in the matter was apparent. He was willing to guarantee the fairest of trials. So, six months after Jesse's death, the surrender of Frank James was arranged.

Major Edwards took Frank James to Jefferson City for his formal surrender at the Capitol. On the train en route, the conductor was co-operative when told the identity of his passenger; he found the two a seat apart, in a place where the outlaw's face would be shaded in such a way that no one would be likely to recognize him. Frank James had an unusual face, sharply triangular: he had been shot three times in the mouth suffering the loss of eight or nine teeth. Consequently, he was easily recognized by anyone who had seen him before.

When they reached Jefferson City, Major Edwards and his charge stopped together at one of the hotels, Frank James registering as "Mr. Winfrey." The next day they went on a sightseeing trip, visiting the Capitol, the Supreme Court building and other points of interest. In the course of their tour, they shook hands with the governor's secretary, two Missouri railroad commissioners and a number of other people. Major Edwards introduced his companion as "Mr. Winfrey," but apparently his identity was well understood. "Mr. Winfrey's" position was peculiar even for "poor old Missouri." There was still an official price of $10,000 on his head. There was also a fund, a little difficult to classify, of $5,000, raised for the purpose of enabling him to surrender with the least possible inconvenience.

The actual surrender took place late that day in Governor Crittenden's office. Frank James handed his revolver and his cartridge belt to the governor, saying it was the first time in twenty-one years that the gun had been out of his possession. The governor shook hands cordially and assured him every consideration of the law. "HE CAME IN" was the headline in the *Missouri Republican*. The surrender occurred on October 5, 1882, and it was often said afterward that the Civil War in Missouri really ended on that date. Even Major Edwards later wrote some editorials favorable to the governor. Governor Crittenden, who had regarded Major Edwards as quite an unreconstructed rebel, noted these editorials in his scrapbook with the remark: "He, too, came in."

Once the formalities of the surrender were over, reporters were called into the governor's office. They described Frank

James as "in excellent health for a man who had been wounded seventeen times. He has a slight scar on his lower lip, which a long, fair mustache hides, and is a little bald, but not from age, being now only thirty-eight . . . soft-spoken, very interesting and intelligent in conversation, a good listener, quite deferential, cool and calm as a statue, and the quickest and deadliest man in a personal encounter between the two oceans."

Far more than his brother Jesse, Frank James was scholarly. He was well read in some of the Elizabethan drama and was able to quote long passages from Shakespeare. As an unofficial hero in Missouri for the next thirty years, he wore well, being quiet but extremely well spoken when he did speak, as appeared in the interviews held on the day of his surrender.

"Are you the noted Frank James?" one of the reporters asked.

"I am Frank James."

"Why did you surrender? No one knew where you were, nor could anyone find out."

"What of that? I was tired of an outlaw's life. I have been hunted for twenty-one years. I have never known a day of perfect peace. It was one long, anxious, inexorable, eternal vigil. When I slept it was in the midst of an arsenal. If I heard dogs bark more fiercely than usual, or the feet of horses in greater volume of sound than usual, I stood to my arms. Have you any idea what a man must endure who leads such a life? No, you cannot. No one can unless he lives it for himself."

He was asked to tell something of his past life.

"No, not now. I have nothing to tell you. The present is mine and the future; let the past go. But this I can say truthfully and without boasting, that I am not nearly as bad as I have been represented to be, and that there is not a drop of blood on my hands. I was a guerilla. I fought the best I knew how under Quantrill, Anderson and Todd; but I never in my life slew an unarmed man or a prisoner."

He was asked if he had perfect confidence in the governor, and replied that if he hadn't he wouldn't be there. Someone asked why he carried a Remington revolver instead of a Smith & Wesson or a Colt, to which he replied:

"Because the Remington is the hardest and surest shooting pistol made, and because it carries exactly the same cartridge as the Winchester rifle does. My armament was two Remingtons and a Winchester rifle. The cartridge of one filled the chamber of the other. You can see why I prefer Remington. There is no confusion of ammunition here. When a man gets into a close, hot fight with a dozen men shooting at him all at once, he must have his ammunition all the same kind."

After the surrender, Frank James was taken by train to Independence, originally with some thought that he might be tried in connection with the death of a Pinkerton detective or on one of two or three other charges in Jackson County. He was under escort rather than under guard, his principal companion being the governor's secretary. In fact, his entire trip across the western half of the state was in the nature of a reception. A newspaper dispatch from Independence, dated October 6, 1882, said:

"At Pleasant Hill the crowd was simply enormous, fully five hundred people being gathered there. So it was the case in Lamonte, Warrensburg and Holden. Not a single harsh word was spoken of the prisoner. The comments were universally in his favor. Arriving at Independence he was met by his old maimed mother, his wife and little boy, Robert. The crowd fell back . . . stout men and sympathetic women wept. He was taken first to the Merchants Hotel in Independence, and there was permitted to receive all his old comrades and friends, probably five hundred in all, among them some of the wealthiest and most influential men in the County." A large dinner was then served.

Following this triumphal tour across the state, this reception and dinner at the Merchants Hotel, Frank James was taken to the Independence jail. This was the only time in their bandit careers that either of the James boys entered a jail. "All I ask is fair treatment and a fair trial," said Frank James. There was talk of getting him out on bond, and a farmer was quoted as saying, "We will make him one for $100,000 in twenty-four hours." A Colonel A. H. Powell, described as "a prominent banker and farmer of Lee's Summit," declared he would go the bond and would get "plenty of others in my town to do likewise." "Twenty prominent men in Independence came in to say the same," wrote the reporter. "It was really surprising to see with what eagerness men rushed forward to do whatever might be required in the case."

For technical reasons Frank James stood trial at Gallatin— not for the old bank robbery there, but in connection with the Winston train robbery which took place in the same county. The courtroom being too small, the trial was held in the Gallatin Opera House. Every man on the jury was a good Democrat, a fact to which the prosecutor could not well object because, although he had made many vigorous attempts to stop the James boys, he was a Democrat too. It was brought out in the trial that when Frank James came back from Arkansas, his wife had shipped her sewing machine north in care of General Jo Shelby, the famous Confederate cavalry hero. General Shelby said that in the battle of Prairie Grove, Arkansas, a band of guerillas that included Frank and Jesse James had saved him from being captured, and that in view of these old ties he had seen no reason to refuse them the usual courtesies.

Frank James said he was not involved in the Winston train

robbery, that he was traveling in Texas at the time. The
Reverend Benjamin Matchett offered some disturbing testimony on this point. The Reverend Mr. Matchett testified that
the day before the Winston train robbery, two men riding
good horses stopped at his home near Winston to have dinner
and feed their animals. One of the men, upon learning that he
was in the home of a minister, started a discussion concerning
the lecturer Robert Ingersoll, and quoted quite ably from
Shakespeare and other poets. That man, the minister said,
was Frank James, the same unsmiling Frank James who was
sitting in the courtroom.

However, the jury took the view that when a reward of
$5,000 has been offered for the conviction of a man, on top of
$5,000 for his capture, a good many witnesses might have a
monetary interest in their testimony, and it could therefore
be disregarded. This suspicion fell especially on the witness
Dick Liddil, who had surrendered to inform.

After four hours' deliberation the jury brought in a verdict
of not guilty. "IT DIDN'T TAKE LONG" was the headline in the
Kansas City *Journal*. A few weeks later the Missouri supreme
court handed down a decision disqualifying the testimony of
any person charged with a felony, which eliminated the
principal witnesses against James and made further trials unnecessary. Usual procedures had been observed to the satisfaction of Governor Crittenden, and Frank James was then
and thereafter as free as any man in Missouri, and as law-
abiding. The surviving guerillas, regarded with awe by the
younger generation, always held annual reunions at Independence. Frank James, who had been at Lawrence, Baxter
Springs, and Centralia, spoke with as much authority as anyone. "Bushwhackers did some bad things, but they never
devastated and ruined a country," he used to say. "When
General Sherman, whom the North worships as a great

Christian general, went on his march to the sea he issued orders that the country be made so desolate that to get over it a crow would have to carry its rations. We did nothing like that. And Order No. 11, Ewing's; I am glad that General Bingham put that on immortal canvas. There is a picture that talks. That order simply ruined hundreds of peaceful homes in western Missouri. I know one man in Jackson County now who made a fortune going around picking up cattle that had been abandoned—a high-toned cattle thief."

The raid on the bank at Northfield had permanently ended the careers of the Younger brothers. Two of the brothers captured there died in prison. The only one who lived to gain his freedom was the eldest, Cole Younger, who emerged after serving twenty-seven years. Frank James was still alive, and for several years he and Cole Younger had a rough-riding tent show which toured the middle states, re-enacting the horsemanship and shooting of the border war and bandit days.

Robert and Charles Ford were charged with murder in the death of Jesse James. Upon pleading guilty, they were sentenced to be hanged. They were immediately pardoned by Governor Crittenden. "The people of Missouri should stand by the Ford boys; their act will redound to the prosperity and advancement of the state," said Governor Crittenden. The Fords received about $1,500 of the reward, the rest going to officers who took part in the negotiations. The brothers made a number of appearances at the Theatre Comique in Kansas City, a heavy detail of police being assigned to protect them; they also had a tent show, exhibiting themselves, the gun with which Jesse James was killed, and other paraphernalia. They were not much of an attraction. No attempt at vengeance on them was ever made. Five years after the death of Jesse, Charley Ford committed suicide at Richmond, Missouri, and, ten years after he pulled the trigger on Jesse, Robert Ford was himself killed by a gunman in an argument over a woman in the Colorado mining town of Creed.

Governor Crittenden considered the suppression of the James boys as the most important act of his administration, and defended his action in the strongest terms. "There was not a horse or an acre of land in the western part of the state whose value was not increased at least thirty-three per cent by the destruction of the James band," he said. But Governor Crittenden's political career was ended. There were so many in Missouri who would never support him again that it was useless to nominate him for an elective office. He himself recorded sadly: "There was a large element in my own party who had more sympathy with such outlaws than with my undertakings to suppress them." Phrasing the difficult proposition as well as anyone could, he added that there were also many who, while not exactly approving of the James boys, yet "acquiesced in their acts with suppressed joy."

Owing to the fact that Jesse James was using the name of Howard when he was shot, impostors to the number of twenty-six arose at different times to claim that he had not been killed, and that they themselves were the real Jesse James. These impostors appeared generally at a good distance from Kansas City, as Jesse James was as well known to the people who filed past his bier as a man could be, and his body was positively identified by five or six war wounds. He was buried in the yard of the Samuels farm, and many people came in later years to see his grave. Nearby, a large coffee-bean tree, sixteen feet around, died because visitors chipped too many souvenirs from it. The outlaw's body was then moved to a cemetery in Kearney. A monument erected to him there was chipped entirely away for souvenirs. The persistence of the souvenir hunters caused Frank James to stipulate in his will that his own body should be cremated and his ashes entombed in a Kansas City bank vault. He lived to a good age. Outsiders sometimes thought it strange that a former bandit was a sort of state hero, and some Missourians wanted to shush-shush this feature of the commonwealth. But he was usually accepted by those who saw his career against the bloody background of the borderland. When he did die there were a number of distinguished men at his funeral. One of them was his old attorney, by this time a Federal judge—Federal Judge John F. Philips—who delivered a moving funeral oration which began with the sentence: "Here lies my friend."

CHAPTER EIGHT

The Iron Horse

COLONEL KERSEY COATES, the man who figured most prominently in Kansas City's development during the years immediately following the Civil War, came from a family of Pennsylvania Quakers. He was a slight, genteel man who wore fair sideburns and a broad black hat. He had taught high school English in the Pennsylvania town of Sadsbury, and he spoke with precision and reserve. At times, he seemed to be standing apart from events. But with his cool gray eyes he saw a great deal which he kept to himself, and which he remembered at the right times.

Pennsylvanians were usually among the relatively few Northerners who were early on the Kansas City scene, because Pittsburgh was at one end of the steamboat line and Kansas City at the other. Colonel Coates came west in 1855, shortly after the opening of the Kansas Territory. By this time he was representing a Philadelphia syndicate of investors, and he intended to go either to Lawrence or Leavenworth in

Kansas. Upon reaching Kansas City, he was so impressed by transportation advantages of the place that he decided, even though the city was located in proslavery Missouri, to remain and do his investing there.

He retained, however, his strongly antislavery views, and he undertook in various ways to champion the Free State cause in Kansas. When Andrew H. Reeder, the first territorial governor of Kansas, was indicted for "treason," on the ground that he refused to recognize the proslavery legislature in Kansas, Colonel Coates rescued him in dramatic fashion. Governor Reeder, like Coates, was a Pennsylvanian. He took refuge with the colonel in Kansas City. Colonel Coates hid him in a back room for several weeks, and then helped him to escape aboard a steamboat in the disguise of an Irish wood-chopper, complete with corncob pipe and an ax and pack.

A painting of Governor Reeder in his disguise, with the corncob pipe between his teeth and the ax and pack slung over his shoulder, hung for fifty years afterward in the Coates House which the colonel built on the Kansas City real estate in which he had invested. In the years after the war, Colonel Coates' record as a vigorous antislavery man enabled him to serve the Kansas City commercial interests as an unofficial ambassador to the Kansans; and his hotel was a headquarters for Kansans coming into the city.

Although he arrived ten years before the railroads, Colonel Coates had been quick to see that Kansas City's transportation advantages involved both steamboats and railroads. On the one hand, there was the Missouri River steamboat landing, which would continue to be important for many years. On the other hand, in the bottom lands along the Kansas River, there was the natural meeting place for the railroads which eventually would run east, west, north, and south through the country. In between the levee district and the bottom lands was the 200-foot West Bluff. Colonel Coates located his interests between the two advantages by buying the real estate on top of the bluff.

In addition to a hotel, he built the spired Coates Opera House which for almost a generation was the city's main claim to culture. His patrons built rambling, full-porched, spired, cupolaed, and ornamented mansions, surrounded by white picket fences. Below the bluff, the railroad and stockyards did locate in the Kansas River bottom lands, and the packing houses were built around the yards. The day came when, from the edge of his prospering real-estate acres, Colonel Coates could look far below on all this industrial and commercial activity that was building the city.

Residents in the colonel's clifftop subdivision were mostly of the northern commercial stamp, and Republican in political leanings. Before the war Colonel Coates had been president of the only Republican Club in western Missouri, the one that rounded up those seventy-two votes for Abraham Lincoln; and after the war he naturally attracted the incoming northern investors and business representatives to his salable acres. In derision, some Democratic phrasemaker looking up from the bottom lands dubbed the colonel's section "Quality Hill." Quality Hill became famous under the name, but locally the name was used by political opponents rather than by residents on the hill.

Originally, horsecars traveled laboriously around the bluff, and plodded through the levee section and up to the main business district and to Quality Hill. Then in the 1880's a half-mile-long trestle was built into the bottom lands from the end of Ninth Street, where the rise of the bluff is one hundred and fifty feet. Today streetcars grind up this trestle, but for thirty years cable cars jerked and slithered up and down its length, giving something of an amusement park effect to

Kansas City's transport system. During the horsecar and the early cable car years, Colonel Coates was the principal figure on Quality Hill.

In the years of the Civil War, Colonel Coates saw the population of Kansas City fall off to about thirty-five hundred, while the population of Leavenworth, Kansas, was swollen to eighteen thousand. The steamboats during the war years usually passed the Kansas City levee and steamed forty miles farther up the river to Leavenworth, which had a large Federal garrison and a safer stem to the wagon trails. After the war, the "era of boats" was ending, and railroads were becoming all-important. Because of its superior size and trade, Leavenworth was selected for important railroad terminals; and for a time Leavenworth instead of Kansas City seemed likely to become the metropolis of the region.

The fate of both Leavenworth and Kansas City hinged on which of them should be the first to get a branch from the railroad that had been built across the northern part of Missouri from Hannibal to St. Joseph. In 1866 alarming reports reached Kansas City that the stockholders of the Hannibal & St. Joe railroad (later absorbed by the Burlington) were planning to push through with a branch to Leavenworth, to build a bridge over the Missouri at Leavenworth, and to make Leavenworth their main terminal. If that happened, ruin was in sight for the real-estate subdivisions which Colonel Coates and others had laid out in Kansas City.

The Hannibal & St. Joe stockholders were in Boston. At the time of the reports, Colonel Coates was in Washington on business. A telegram was sent which caused him to hurry up to Boston to investigate. Upon reaching Boston, Colonel Coates learned that the stockholders had already voted in favor of the Leavenworth branch, and that a delegation from Leavenworth had been called in to negotiate the contract.

However, the signatures had not yet been affixed and the bargain had not been sealed. With decisive energy, Colonel Coates claimed that the vote of the stockholders was invalid because of a previous agreement for a branch to Kansas City. In truth, the Missouri legislature in 1857 had granted a charter to the "Kansas City, Galveston & Lake Superior Railroad Company" to build fifteen hundred miles of road. There had been some amusement over the charter because, although granted by the Missouri legislature, only one hundred and twenty-nine of the specified miles were in Missouri; and it had been generally understood that the Kansas City projectors of this great system would for the present be content if they could find means to build fifty-two miles of branch line. But the charter *did* include the Hannibal & St. Joe branch, and there *had* been talk that the Hannibal & St. Joe company would help financially with its building. That was the previous agreement to which Colonel Coates now referred.

Regarding the terms of the agreement, he was indefinite. He said he could think of only one man in the Hannibal company who would remember them, and that man at the moment was in Paris. Nevertheless, he succeeded in convincing the stockholders that final decision should be postponed until the relative merits of Kansas City and Leavenworth had been investigated.

The stockholders left the decision to their western division manager, who went out and looked over the ground at Leavenworth and at Kansas City. The main routes to the West were accessible from Leavenworth, and that town had other advantages which might have enabled it to take the lead. But the manager was even more impressed with the advantages at Kansas City, where the peculiar junction of the rivers and grades made it possible to build a "water level" road in any direction required. So the manager agreed to shift the branch to Kansas City—with the stipulation that congressional authority must first be obtained for a bridge across the still unbridged Missouri.

Another telegram was sent to Washington, this time to Colonel Robert T. Van Horn, the first editor of the Kansas City *Journal,* who was serving in Congress. Like Colonel Coates, Colonel Van Horn was a Pennsylvanian. A friend of Van Horn's, also a Pennsylvanian, was the chairman of the House Committee of Post Offices and Post Roads. This committee had approved a bill for a bridge across the Mississippi at Quincy, Illinois. The two Pennsylvanians went into conference, and both arrived early for the next session of the House. Congressman Van Horn asked for unanimous consent to dispense with the clerk's usual reading of the journal. The committee chairman then called up his bill for a bridge across the Mississippi at Quincy, Illinois. Noting that no member from Kansas was yet present, Congressman Van Horn attached an amendment for a bridge across the Missouri at Kansas City. Before opposition could develop, the bill with its rider was passed. The same lightning-like legislative procedure was repeated in the Senate, and within a few days the bridge at Kansas City was assured.

The promise of the bridge assured the future of Kansas City. With the release of materials after the war, the railroads were advancing with great strides over all parts of the country. Yet nowhere along the twisting course of the Missouri was there a bridge to take the railroads across. As soon as the bridge at Kansas City was assured, the different railroads laid plans to route traffic in that direction. The bridge was built by Octave Chanute, who also built the first New York elevated lines, and who practiced with gliders on the sand dunes of

Indiana. It was a major engineering achivement in a day when the principal bridge-building materials were timber and masonry. When it was completed three years later in 1869— the year the golden spike was driven which united the coasts by rail—there were four railroads running on one side of the Missouri and three on the other. Seven railroad lines were thus connected by the bridge at Kansas City.

While the bridge was being built, the railroad shops were also going up. Kansas City's population increased to nearly forty thousand. More than that number of people were present to celebrate the opening of the bridge on July 4, 1869. High over their heads floated two large balloons; pride in local manufacturing was beginning to be evidenced, and each balloon bore a sign: FILLED WITH OUR OWN GAS, MANUFACTURED HERE.

The building of the Hannibal Bridge was the turning point in Kansas City's history. During 1869, the year of the bridge, 260,000 settlers passed through the city. Forty thousand came by steamboat, 70,000 by rail and 150,000 by wagon. The post–Civil War migration, now breaking through at a number of points, far surpassed anything that had gone before.

Kansas City soon began getting a backflow of livestock and of various products brought by the arrival of the railroads and settlers. One of the first "products" to arrive in quantity was the bones of the disappearing buffalo, which were used in making carbon, buttons, and fertilizer. A number of railroads in the years after the war listed buffalo bones as their principal item of eastbound freight, and one later estimate stated that the skeletons of thirty million buffalo had been hauled in from the plains.

The Texas Longhorns were also early in the picture. During the Civil War, the herds of Texas range cattle had greatly increased, and after the war the exhausted South provided no market for them. The Texans were "cattle poor." In 1866, nearly a quarter of a million Longhorns were driven north across the Red River. These herds ran into fenced territory in Missouri, where the farmers feared they would damage property and would spread Spanish fever among domestic cattle. The Missouri farmers in 1866 formed parties which broke up the Texas herds. The cattle were scattered, and most of them fell into the hands of rustlers. In spite of the first year's debacle, however, more thousands of Texas cattle again in 1867 were driven north in search of a market.

The problem was to find a town at which the Texas cattle could reach the railroads without crossing fenced territory. Since only the eastern and least desertlike third of Kansas had been settled before the war, there was still open territory south of Abilene, Kansas, which was one hundred and fifty miles west of Kansas City. Abilene therefore was selected as the first buying point, and in four years half a million cattle were driven to that town. As the country became more settled and fenced, the buying point was successively moved to the west and south, to Ellsworth, Newton, Wichita, Great Bend and Dodge City, Kansas. Although settled by reformers and with state prohibition on its books as early as 1880, Kansas thus acquired all the hard-drinking and fast-shooting atmosphere of these cow towns. The trailing of cattle, across Indian country between Texas and Kansas, continued for nearly twenty years, during which five or six million head were driven north.

Kansas City was the nearest control station for the different systems of railroads, which were fed by spur lines from the cow towns. During the trailing years, nearly all the cattle were brought there for transhipment. They were unloaded, fed, watered and reloaded in the bottom lands along the Kansas River, the beginning of the Kansas City stockyards.

The West Bottoms thus became a livestock as well as a railroad center.

The atmosphere of the cow towns was also brought into Kansas City, which became a "capital of cow towns." Wyatt Earp, Bat Masterson, Doc Holliday, "Wild Bill" Hickok and other well-known gunmen were all familiar figures. These gunmen were the celebrities of the day, and their personalities were much better known than those of the residents on Quality Hill. "Wild Bill" Hickok, who had been a Kansas scout during the war, lived three years in Kansas City, and walked every day to play faro at the Marble Hall. He never shot anyone here, though it was reputed he had eighty-two notches on his gun from exploits elsewhere.

In the levee district there was a row of lesser saloons known as "Battle Row." But befitting a "capital of cow towns," Kansas City offered something more luxurious than the usual pine-board bars. The leading gambling places were the Marble Hall and the House of Lords. They were housed in brick buildings, furnished with thick carpets, crystal chandeliers and mahogany bars. In addition to gambling, they offered the best of food, drink, and entertainment, and they were patronized by a large part of the citizenry.

Steamboating on the Missouri continued for ten or twelve years after the coming of the railroads, when the navigation of that shifting and treacherous river was then given up. In 1880, only the ferry boat *Annie Cade* and an occasional sternwheeler were still using the levee. Instead of facing north on the levee, the city now faced west on the railroad center. The main business district was formed at the "junction," the intersection of streets from the old levee district with the Ninth Street line to the West Bottoms. In 1880, the city was still in the horsecar stage. Most of the gunmen celebrities had moved farther west, but the gambling houses were still thriving. The population had risen to fifty-five thousand, and the city was on the verge of another period of rapid development, the real-estate boom of the eighties.

In that quiet year of 1880, John C. McCoy, the founder of the city, was growing elderly and was writing his recollections at his home in the still-separate town of Westport. "We never dreamed we were founding a city," was the thought that frequently recurred in McCoy's reminiscence of the fur-trading days. Many people became weary of hearing the old-timers talk of the old days; but because of his special position as the founder of the city, McCoy was able to get his recollections printed in the back pages of the Kansas City *Journal*, under such headings as: "OUR OLD-TIMER WRITES AGAIN."

Sometimes McCoy was optimistic concerning the future of the city, and concerning the developments which he said had made the country "a gridiron of railroads." At other times he thought there had been better days. Into one of his articles he put a good deal of melancholy feeling. "There is no longer any Far West," he wrote. "It is gone like the misty clouds of morning. The iron horse has swept it across that broad, mythical Desert, over the snow-capped Rocky Mountains, across the canyons, the hills and the valleys a thousand miles, across the Sierras and down the wide slopes of the Pacific; and it is lost forever where the broad sun gently sinks down in those limitless waters beyond."

CHAPTER NINE

The Crystal Gazer

EIGHTEEN HUNDRED AND EIGHTY was a pivotal year for Kansas City: In the eighties the scene changed rapidly and began to take on something of its present aspects and dimensions. Forces had gathered for a chain of booms which struck also in other cities of the West, including Chicago, Omaha, Denver, San Francisco and Los Angeles. A new generation of Westerners, sons and daughters of the pioneers who moved westward before and after the Civil War, had grown up. The immigrants from the East poured into the cities instead of onto the land. Attention was now on commercial organization; and in the process the old frontier character of the towns disappeared.

The new order of things was expressed in the Johnson anti-gambling law, which went into effect in Missouri in 1881. That was a sad day for the old-time gamblers in Kansas City. Bob Potee, a faro dealer, distinguished-appearing in his formal gambling clothes, could not accept living under the changed regime. He walked into the river until his silk hat floated, and he was carried away by the current. He left a note for Charlie Bassett, owner of the Marble Hall gambling house, asking him to "plant me decent"; and Bassett arranged for six tall gamblers to carry his casket down the church aisle. But Charlie Bassett himself failed rapidly after his Marble Hall was closed; his eyesight dimmed until he couldn't see a card, and soon he too was dead. Faro (named for the pictures of the pharaohs on the backs of the cards) was also dead. It was a game which had become popular on the steamboats, and although gambling returned, this game was never revived.

In 1882, Jesse James was killed and Frank James surrendered. Missouri assumed a more staid and settled character. On the plains of Kansas, the scene was equally changed. Twenty years after the Civil War, the trailing of cattle was ending, and the scrawny, long-legged, light-footed Texas Longhorns had almost disappeared. They had been replaced gradually by low-slung, white-faced Herefords. As early as 1880, there were a million domestic cattle in Kansas. Farmers came to Kansas City both to sell their livestock and to buy range cattle for feeding, and the stockyards underwent a rapid growth.

The refrigerator car, invented in 1867, was coming into use, and the cities of the East were filled with meat-hungry people. Packing houses, connected by long, covered chutes, ranged themselves around the stockyards, which eventually extended to one hundred and seventy-five acres of concrete-floored pens. In the eighties, the million-a-year marks for cattle and hog receipts were passed, and the city's main activity was permanently fixed.

Banks were established on the loans farmers needed to buy cattle for feeding. Soap and glue factories took their place in industry. Originally, because there was timber along the railroads stretching to the south, Kansas City became a lumber center, and this position it continued to hold even after the logging swung up into the Northwest. It also became the leading distributor of agricultural implements. The mail-order business got an early start through newspaper advertisements. One advertisement made a combination offer of a watch, a rocking chair and four quarts of whisky for $3.18, collect.

In the eighties also, the real-estate boom struck Kansas City, a boom such as the city never saw before or again. It was said at one time that if all the platted land had been occupied, the city would have been larger than London. Horsemen galloped through the streets announcing auctions of lots, and buyers were trotted in carriages to distant points. One buyer arrived at midnight, insisted on being taken out at once, and after two hours of inspection by moonlight bought twenty acres of Kansas City lots. Westport was engulfed and the expansion reached the borders of Independence. Cable cars replaced horsecars to serve the outlying sections. Real-estate transfers which had amounted to five million dollars in 1880 climbed to nearly one hundred million in 1887, and the suburban turnover added another thirty-nine million. The population which had been fifty-five thousand in 1880 was tripled in ten years.

Kansans as well as Missourians joined in the movement toward the city. There were some Kansans still who couldn't look a Missourian in the eye, and Missourians who couldn't look a Kansan in the eye, and old people on both sides who would not step across the border; but these were a minority. Approximately three-fourths of all the migration into the city after the Civil War was Northern in character, and a large part of this was from Kansas.

Independence on the east, not growing much, remained in

all respects a Southern town. Kansas City, Kansas, attached on the west, was entirely Northern in character. Kansas City itself, in between, contained both Northern and Southern elements. As the migration to the city continually became larger the old Southern element, sometimes called the "cat-fish aristocracy" because its members had come up the river in the steamboat days, was reduced to a minority—in the city itself, though not in the Missouri countryside.

Politically, because of the lines on which the Democratic party developed nationally, the Southerners were allied with labor and minority groups in such a way as, usually, to figure prominently in the control of the city's politics. Commercially, the Northern investors and organizers were more in evidence. And commercially, for a number of reasons, the city looked more toward Kansas than toward Missouri. One reason was that St. Louis, from the other side of the state, spread its influence over a good part of Missouri. Another was that Kansas City, at the mouth of the Kansas River bisecting that state, was the natural receiving point for Kansas products. A third reason was that Kansas, after the eclipse of Leavenworth, did not develop a city of competing size. Kansas City, Kansas, became that state's largest city, but it never developed much of a business district because its residents preferred to do their downtown shopping on the better-stocked Missouri side.

Kansas agriculture suffered some hard early years. There were a number of drouths, during which "Great American Desert" seemed an apt description of the country. Then in 1874, swarms of grasshoppers (Rocky Mountain locusts) descended on Kansas and western Missouri like a biblical plague. These grasshoppers were so numerous that they were sometimes piled up several feet deep on the ground. After eating everything in sight, they burrowed into the ground to lay millions of eggs which incubated during the winter, and the plague threatened to be equally bad in 1875. Eastern cities were sending trainloads of relief supplies to the Kansans, and it appeared that a desolation might sweep over all of the state.

But the Rocky Mountain locusts are curious creatures. Their young do not care for the lands in which they are propagated. Because of an instinctive urge to migrate, the swarms usually seek a new location as soon as the second generation acquires wings. In 1875 the governor of Missouri had proclaimed a day of prayer for deliverance from the grasshoppers. In a somewhat disconcerting turn of events, the creatures did not wait for the day of prayer, but took off in advance of it and flew away, in a series of dense clouds that darkened the sky. Years later, Speaker Champ Clark of Missouri sometimes chuckled about "the year Governor Hardin prayed the grasshoppers out of Kansas."

During the grasshopper plague, five or six thousand Mennonite immigrants arrived from Russia. They brought with them a variety of hard wheat called "Red Turkey," or "Turkey Red." This wheat was sown in the fall and harvested in June and July, after having had the full advantage of the spring moisture. The grain proved to be an excellent producer for Kansas, the climate of which is similar to that of the Russian steppes. With other improvements, Kansas agriculture was placed on a sound basis and Kansas then took the position which it has since held, as the leading wheat-producing state in the country. In the eighties, the Kansas farmers were already producing ten times as much wheat as could be consumed at home.

The wheat was coming into Kansas City; but in spite of the thriving railroad and stockyard activity in the West Bottoms, Kansas City was providing few facilities for handling grain. There was only one elevator, operating part time. Sometimes the wheat brought a dollar a bushel, but more often it was down to thirty-five cents. It was usually shipped eastward without being unloaded, a discouraging process, since the freight rate to the east coast was twenty-six cents a hundred pounds (15.6 cents a bushel), which was often nearly half the price of the wheat. So, in spite of their heavy production of wheat, the Kansas farmers were suffering hard times. At this point there appeared on the scene a young man named Arthur E. Stilwell, who became known in America as the "boy railroad president," and who eventually could boast that he had built more miles of railroad than any other man alive.

Arthur E. Stilwell came from Rochester, New York, and reached Kansas City in 1888, at the age of twenty-seven. He had already made a rather spectacular career as an insurance salesman, and had saved $25,000. Because he admired his grandfather, one of the builders of the Erie Canal and the New York Central railroad, he had from his youth cherished an ambition to build a railroad in the West. He did not at first see any possibility of raising the long-term capital necessary for railroad building; so he organized a trust company, and made a start building low-priced houses in Kansas City.

From the first his activities created a stir. Stilwell was a handsome fellow, with luxuriant sideburns, and he had a flare for publicity. Upon his arrival in Kansas City, he called in reporters and announced that he would build houses and sell them to the working people, in instalments which would be less than the rent they were paying, with "all debts canceled in case of death." This unusual form of financing came to him because he had invented an insurance endowment policy. He patterned his house-selling along the same lines. A down payment of 20 per cent was required, the rest to be paid in instalments over ten years, and, in the event of death, the debt was canceled and the house deeded to the buyer's heirs like an insurance payment. "You can live in your endowment policy and raise chickens in its back yard," was his company's slogan.

The Kansas City bankers were reluctant to come in with him, so Stilwell went to Philadelphia. He obtained lists of the directors of a number of banking and manufacturing companies, made a special list of men who appeared as directors of several firms, and picked a name by lot. The name was William Waterall, a leading paint manufacturer. Stilwell succeeded in seeing Waterall and convinced him that the house-building idea was sound. Waterall introduced him to important leaders among Philadelphia bankers, A. J. Drexel, E. T. Stotesbury, and others. He raised $300,000 in Philadelphia. Whereupon the Kansas City bankers also came in with him. Within a year he was the head of a million-dollar company, and was building houses in Lincoln, Nebraska, Wichita, Kansas, and St. Joseph, Missouri, as well as in Kansas City.

But he was still interested in fulfilling his youthful ambition to build a railroad. One day a friend mentioned that he was unable to raise money to build a suburban belt railroad in the eastern and southern parts of Kansas City, and was about to lose his franchise for the project. Stilwell immediately dropped everything and began raising money for the Kansas City Suburban Belt. He approached the same bankers who had supported his house-building plan, and soon had $350,000. Tracks were laid in the East Bottoms along the Blue River, and a $65,000 station was erected at the foot of Wyandotte Street. Stilwell's depot was one of the lesser railroad buildings in the town, but he named it the "Grand Central Station"; and his branch to Independence, which included sixteen reverse curves, he called "The Kansas City–Independence Air Line."

To create business for his Air Line, he built a park—Fairmont Park—between Kansas City and Independence. The park was filled with beautiful fountains over which multicolored lights were played; it provided a dining room seating six hundred people and a lecture hall seating two thousand. Stilwell arranged for chautauquas and lectures to be held here, far enough from town so that people would have to use his railroad. The park was a great success, and on some days the railroad took as many as 15,000 passengers to and from its grounds.

In spite of this development, however, his Suburban Belt nearly came to grief. The reason was that the line had been built in the East Bottoms, where there had been no industrial development. All the packing houses, the stockyards, the railroad shops, and the main railroad station were in the West Bottoms, along the Kansas River. For Stilwell's Belt line to connect with the packing houses, and with the seventeen railroads entering Kansas City, it was essential that the line be extended into the West Bottoms.

Kansas City's West Bluff faces west on the Kansas River, but extends to the Missouri River at the point of the old levee. The smaller north bluffs which have since been graded away, formerly also came out to this point, or receded back from it. The two systems of bluffs thus formed a rough wedge, pointed toward the levee, the wedge also dividing the east and west bottom lands. In McCoy's day there was barely room for a single horseman to pass between the end of the bluffs and the edge of the river. In Stilwell's time, the space had been widened enough to accommodate the double tracks of the Missouri Pacific railroad. But there was no room for additional tracks. Moreover, Stilwell's Grand Central Station at the foot of Wyandotte Street was one hundred feet above the level of the bottoms. By no acceptable railroad grade could the line be extended from there to the West Bottoms, which were only a few hundred yards away. His surveyors gave up the problem, and an expert to whom he paid $100 a day was unable to solve it.

Then Stilwell had his first vision. As he later explained the experience, he was wrought up over the problem; his mind continued to work after he had fallen asleep, and when he awoke the problem was solved. In his sleep, he saw a spur of his line extended westward on elevated tracks from a lower level at the foot of Grand Avenue. On these elevated tracks it would reach a point from which it could be projected past the end of the bluffs, across the Missouri Pacific tracks and into the West Bottoms by means of a bridge. Upon checking with his surveyors, he found that this could be done and was, in fact, the solution.

A part of Stilwell's vision indicated that the ground in the West Bottoms, where he would need to sink a pier for his bridge, had been owned by Colonel Kersey Coates. This did not at first appear to be the case. The Missouri Pacific claimed to own the land, and would not sell it to him at any price. Colonel Coates had died. His heirs said that they did not own the property, and that they never had owned it. Nevertheless, Stilwell took an option to buy at $15,000 an acre from the Coates heirs, if he could show that they owned the property. The option was, to say the least, unusual, since it proposed to buy property which the Coates heirs were sure they did not own.

Stilwell then had the titles searched. He found that in building along the river past the bluff, the Missouri Pacific had taken a fifty-foot right-of-way. In branching to the south-west, the railroad had pre-empted another fifty-foot strip. In between the two rights-of-way was a wedge of ground not covered by either. The wedge of ground was exactly where he needed to sink his pier for the bridge. And, sure enough, it had belonged to Kersey Coates, the Quaker colonel of Quality Hill, and therefore was the rightful property of his heirs. The remarkable character of this incident was fully in consonance with the whole of Stilwell's career from that day forward.

Once his Belt line was extended into the West Bottoms, it became a terminal railroad system, and came to be regarded as one of the best in the country. Stilwell had sold $1,000 bonds for $666, and had given $2,000 in stock with each bond—$3,000 in face value for $666—making the bonds a very profitable investment if the enterprise succeeded. In its third year, his suburban line paid $2 a share on its bonus stock. His credit with the bankers was excellent, and he was eager to extend the line. When someone suggested laying tracks to the coal fields at Hume, Missouri, he pointed out that there was much better coal a little farther on at Pittsburg, Kansas. When the tracks had reached Pittsburg, he suggested going on to the great lead and zinc business at Joplin, Missouri. "What I was really thinking about all the time," Stilwell said later, "was building a railroad to the sea, but I was afraid if I sprang it on the other people at that early stage they might object."

When the track had reached Joplin, Stilwell called attention to the plight of the Kansas farmers. Low-priced wheat was being shipped fourteen hundred miles to the east coast for export, when there were ports on the Gulf of Mexico which were six hundred miles closer. "The farmers are selling their corn at fifteen cents and their wheat at thirty-five cents,"

Stilwell said. "The Kansas City packing houses are not doing anything like what they should. And why? Simply because we are bottled up in the hinterland, with no outlet to the seaboard, except at ruinous rates. A direct railroad to the Gulf will bring the West the greatest prosperity it has ever known, and the men who build it will go down in history."

The line to the sea was accordingly started. It had only reached Siloam Springs, Arkansas, less than two hundred miles south of Kansas City, when the country was struck by the panic of 1893. The Wabash, Union Pacific and other railroads went into receivership, and further building seemed out of the question.

Then it came to Stilwell in another vision that if he went to Amsterdam he could sell $3,000,000 worth of securities. Why the place should have been Amsterdam, he could not say, as he had been there only three days on a vacation. Nevertheless, despite every assurance that no one in Europe was buying American securities, he set off for Amsterdam. Once there, he interviewed all the Dutch bankers and advertised a $3,000,000 issue; but in three weeks he did not succeed in interesting a single banker, nor did he sell so much as one bond.

These setbacks convinced Stilwell that he was using the wrong methods. He remembered that once, on board a ship, he had met a man who was from Amsterdam. He could not remember the man's name, but recalled that he was a coffee merchant. He went to the coffee exchange, and found his friend. The friend protested that there was no relation between selling coffee and selling railroad securities, but Stilwell signed him on a $15,000 contract to help him with his task. He then leased a four-story building in Amsterdam, and fitted it up with offices.

The coffee merchant proved to have what Stilwell needed:

a contact with all the financial writers in Amsterdam. Stilwell again advertised his $3,000,000 issue, and to the accompaniment of some notice in the financial pages he sold a few bonds. The response, however, was meager. In studying the advertisement, Stilwell noted a line which said, "No subscriptions for less than twenty thousand guilders received." He changed that to read "one thousand guilders." Then he reinserted the advertisement and gave out a statement to the effect that he had always intended to let the public in on the issue, and that the restriction to twenty thousand guilders had been inserted without his approval. This time the publicity he received was adequate. The entire $3,000,000 issue was subscribed in twenty-seven minutes, and in one hour went to a premium of 25 per cent on the market.

Financial writers said his activities in Amsterdam had helped turn gold shipments back toward American shores. In the depression year of 1893, his railroad laid a third of the country's new mileage. In building toward the principal division point in Arkansas, the future town of Mena, Stilwell hit upon the idea of laying track at a rate of "a mile a day for forty days." It would have been equally easy, he later said, to lay a mile and a half of track a day, but "a mile a day for forty days" *sounded* faster. The newspapers carried daily reports on his "race against time." The publicity attracted town-settlers who preceded the railroad in wagons, and for them Stilwell operated lunch wagons along the route, with tents to accommodate sleepers at twenty-five cents a night. There were already 1,000 people camped on the site of Mena before the railroad reached there. So many of them were from Iowa, Minnesota, Wisconsin, and Nebraska that when the time came, they elected a Republican congressman in a district where few people had ever expected to see a Republican in the flesh. Stilwell claimed to have made the first dent in the "Solid South." The town was named "Mena" after the Dutch contraction for Queen Wilhelmina. His Amsterdam friend, the coffee merchant, was named de Geoijen, which in Dutch was pronounced something like "de Hooyan," and which was Americanized into De Queen. As the latter, it survived as the name of another good-sized Arkansas town.

The line to the Gulf was to have ended at Shreveport, and to have used the tracks of other railroads to Houston, Galveston, New Orleans, and other points. Stilwell had already built the Union Station at Shreveport, and was president of the Shreveport terminal railroad system. Then it came to him in still another of his visions that he should end the line on a lake, and build a canal to the Gulf, thus acquiring a landlocked harbor as protection against the severe storms of the Gulf coast.

"This was the weirdest of all the hunches I have ever had," said Stilwell. "For days I had been thinking of little else than the fact that the time was rapidly approaching when I should have my termini on the Gulf of Mexico, and I suppose the constant pounding over this might have been responsible. At any rate, I became possessed of an overpowering fear that we were planning wrongly this time in relying on the coast of the Gulf of Mexico as our principal terminus, because of the storms of tremendous violence that lashed those shores at times.

"The whole incident was a repetition of that earlier occasion when my mind had kept on working after I had fallen asleep, and I had solved the problem of how we could run a line from the East to the West Bottoms. An intuitive sense told me to abandon the entire project and look to a more north-easterly portion of the Texas coast for the end of our line to deep water. I did so, and there occurred to me a picture of a city with a population of about 100,000 persons on the bank of Lake Sabine, which could be connected with the Gulf by means of a canal about seven miles long. Here, in this landlocked harbor, safe from the most devastating storms, we could erect elevators and piers and create a port for the shipment of the western farmers' export grain."

Stilwell visited Lake Sabine, and although he had never been in the region before, he "found the whole layout as I expected it to be." The lake could be connected with the Gulf by a canal about seven miles long. The land on the north bank of Lake Sabine was open grazing country, easily purchased. Stilwell bought forty thousand acres, at seven dollars an acre. "I am going to build a great city there and call it Port Arthur after my first name," he said. He laid out four thousand acres of the town, naming the principal thoroughfare "Stilwell Boulevard." The lots sold rapidly, and he had $135,000 in hand from the lots before he made the first payment on the land. He had an excess of 36,000 acres of land, so he employed a soil taster to see how the land might be used. The soil taster said he had never tasted soil that was better for growing rice. Stilwell then formed the Nederland Rice Farm Company, and interested his Dutch friends in sending over a colony to raise rice. The soil did prove excellent for rice, and the Nederland farming company, capitalized at $300,000, in a few years paid $2,000,000 in dividends.

The flow of Kansas wheat which had been eastward, was turned southward. Port Arthur, Texas, became the country's second largest port for grain exports, second only to New York. Kansas City, with elevators located on Stilwell's Suburban Belt, became the country's leading winter wheat market. As many as four or five thousand carloads of wheat arrived on some June and July days, and sometimes twenty-five thousand carloads stood in the yards. There were other railroads reaching the Gulf, but Stilwell's direct line shortened the distance by 114 miles, and reduced the freight on export grain from twenty-six to sixteen cents a hundred. His line eventually became the Kansas City Southern, one of the most profitable railroads. After the various consolidations of the railroads had taken place, the Southern was the only major railroad still retaining its main headquarters in Kansas City. In banquet speeches, Stilwell was credited with adding eighty-eight cents an acre to the producing value of every farm in Kansas, $10 an acre to fixed land values, increasing the Kansas City bank turnover by 150 per cent, and adding 50 per cent to the city's population.

In spite of the success of the railroad and the improved economic conditions that resulted, Stilwell lost control of the Kansas City Southern almost as soon as it was completed. All his hunches had turned out so well that he had become a thorough believer in visions, and was inclined to base major decisions on dreams of the previous night. This may have caused some of the directors to look upon him skeptically. He himself, on one occasion, referred to "the theory that seemed to be popular among people who knew me; namely, that I had a screw loose somewhere." In any case, in 1900 he was voted out of the presidency of the Southern.

Only a few days after losing his post, Stilwell was embarked on another railroad-building project. He first announced somewhat mysteriously that he would bring the Pacific Ocean 400 miles closer to Kansas City, with a port only 200 miles west of Salt Lake City. "I have designed a railroad 1,700 miles long which will not only bring the Pacific Ocean four hundred miles closer, but will place us 1,600 miles nearer to Central and South America than San Francisco is," he said. "When the railroad is finished and in operation, the population of

Kansas City will be increased in the same way it has grown through the influence of the Kansas City Southern."

Stilwell's second project was for the Kansas City, Mexico & Orient, known as the Orient line. The plan was to build a railroad on the shortest line from Kansas City to the Pacific. The shortest line ran southwest through Kansas, through Indian country that was to become part of Oklahoma, through the Texas panhandle, and through old Mexico to a little port called Topolobampo on the Gulf of California. Apart from being the shortest line to the Pacific, its port, as Stilwell said, would be much closer to South America. It would be only 200 miles west of Salt Lake City, but more than 1,000 miles south.

Everyone who had invested money with Stilwell in house-building, in the Suburban Belt, and in the Kansas City Southern had made big profits. His credit with the bankers was still good. Dr. W. S. Woods, a former physician who was head of Kansas City's Bank of Commerce and the leading financier of the West at the time, had made a profit of $300,000 from Stilwell's operations. So Dr. Woods came into the Orient plan to the extent of $100,000, and brought in his associates for another $400,000.

Stilwell then set off for Mexico, to obtain permission to build through that country. Dr. Woods' bank telegraphed the governors of middle-western states that he was on a mission of importance to the West. When Stilwell reached President Diaz of Mexico, he found that he had been preceded by telegrams of recommendation from the governors of Minnesota, Wisconsin, Nebraska, Kansas, Iowa, Missouri, Texas, Arkansas and Louisiana. President Diaz was very cordial. He granted a concession to build the railroad, and granted five thousand dollars a mile for construction purposes. Stilwell later used his connections to sell securities in all parts of the country and abroad, and altogether raised twenty million dollars for the Orient line.

However, he had failed to consider how he would build across Mexico's section of the Continental Divide, a range of mountains rising 8,300 feet and of a baffling terrain for railroad construction. This proved to be what the English call a "cropper," on a grand scale. Stilwell did not know until he reached Mexico City that General Ulysses S. Grant, after he was President, had attempted to build a railroad through that section of Mexico, and had concluded that its construction was impossible. When he did learn of Grant's experience, it did not make the slightest difference to Stilwell. He simply began laying track. and assumed that the problem of getting through the mountains would be solved in due time. But in twelve years of track-laying, the problem was not solved. Consequently, although he built more than a thousand miles of the Orient line, it was in three unconnected sections. Two of the sections were in Mexico, one on either side of the mountains, and the third section was in the United States. It was a railroad, as was sometimes said, that did not start anywhere and did not end anywhere. After twelve years, Stilwell thought he had solved the problem of the mountains; but by that time a receivership had caught up with his railroad, and he was forced out.

Nevertheless, the three separate sections of the Orient continued to operate, in receivership. The section which was in the United States ran from Wichita, Kansas, through Oklahoma and to Alpine, Texas, a distance of seven hundred miles. There were 119 towns along this stretch of the Orient, most of them wholly dependent on the Orient for rail transportation. Interested parties and the government came to the railroad's rescue from time to time, to keep it in operation. In his later years, Stilwell could say that he had built 2,300 miles of railroad, over all of which trains were running. And, although the $20,000,000 that went into the Orient was lost, he could say that investors of $40,000,000 in his other enterprises had realized $160,000,000 in dividends and profits.

As Stilwell grew older, he became more certain that he had been the recipient of true visions. If he had held to his original plan of building the Kansas City Southern only to Shreveport, and using the tracks of other railroads from that point, his principal outlet to the sea (before the development of the Houston ship channel) would have been Galveston, Texas. After Galveston, in 1900, was laid waste by a tidal wave in which five thousand people perished, it seemed to Stilwell that he had forseen this tidal wave. He wrote in later years that it was the coming tidal wave that had caused him to establish Port Arthur. Whatever may be said of Stilwell's later spiritualistic leanings, the fact remains that his visions, or intuition, or hunches, were repeatedly, although not invariably, sound, and that as a result he left his mark on the face of the earth.

Even his last hunch was sound. Its vindication did not come in time for him or his investors to benefit from his enterprise, and it did not come in the way he anticipated, but eventually it came. After the Orient had been years in receivership, oil was discovered along its tracks, in Oklahoma and Texas, as well as elsewhere in the Southwest. Kansas City was outside the oil region itself, but as the rail center for the Southwest the city benefited from the development. Oil added the last of the city's several economic layers, bringing hundreds of tank cars to fill its yards, large refineries to the vicinity, and the homes of oil magnates to the south part of town. Oil also gave new value to the Orient railroad, which became a carrier of crude petroleum.

In 1928, the Santa Fe railroad, the largest carrier of

petroleum in the country, decided to buy and absorb the Orient, thus acquiring its track, equipment and business. The Santa Fe paid $414.50 a share for the Orient's stock, a total price exceeding $14,000,000. By that time something more than a majority of the reorganized Orient's stock, acquired when it was of dubious value, was in the hands of W. T. Kemper, Kansas City banker. A court had awarded Kemper 15,000 shares of the stock in compensation for his services as receiver of the railroad. So Stilwell's old, decrepit and disconnected Orient railroad became the main foundation stone in the Kemper fortune, the largest family fortune in Kansas City today.

CHAPTER TEN

Baron of Brush Creek

DURING THE EIGHTIES, William Rockhill Nelson, founder of the Kansas City *Star,* was lifted to the highest position of eminence and influence in the city and in the territory it served. Because he arrived when the city was still in the unpaved, horsecar stage, and lived on through the early phases of the "skyscraper" fever, the statement has often been made of him as of some Roman emperors: that he "found a city in mud and left it in marble."

Nelson was born near Fort Wayne, Indiana. The families from which he came, the Nelsons and the Rockhills, were two of the wealthiest clans in the Hoosier state. From his earliest years he knew broad acres, spacious rooms, walnut stairways and marble fireplaces. Both the Nelson and Rockhill farms were show places, the subjects of admiring articles in the early agricultural magazines. His father, who was from Dutchess County, New York, was a slender, cultivated man who prided

himself on his library, his Jeffersonian principles and his horti-
culture.

The boy William Rockhill Nelson, however, resembled his
father in few respects. He grew up short-legged and massive in
the waist, and from the stories told around Fort Wayne must
have been a source of many headaches for his father. He refused to attend school, and at the age of ten was discovered
leading an assault with overripe fruit and melancholy eggs
that drove a political speaker from a platform. When he was
fifteen his father sent him to Notre Dame college, then noted
for its strict discipline, and there he attended for two turbulent
seasons.

One of the Notre Dame professors, as an act of discipline,
assigned him to memorize a section of Pollock's *Course of
Time*. Although not usually studious, Nelson was anxious to
show how little he thought of the punishment, and memorized
the lines so quickly that the professor assigned him another
section to learn. In a rage over this treatment, he drove a long
nail through the book, bent the nail over, and with the book
thus sealed tossed it defiantly on the professor's desk. The head
of the college held that he was perhaps justified in his action,
ruling that he had done his task and should not have been
assigned more work. But such incidents were too frequent, and
after two years the school declined to accept his further
enrollment.

At seventeen he was in charge of his father's farm. He
reached the age of twenty-one in 1862, but took no part in the
Civil War. After the war his father financed him in raising
sea-island cotton on a plantation scale, near Savannah,
Georgia, but that venture collapsed the following year when
the price of cotton fell. He returned to Fort Wayne, and went
into contracting. He also became interested in politics. He
bought into the Fort Wayne *Sentinel*, at first only for the

political influence it would give him. Then his contracting business failed, when a bridge was washed out, and he devoted himself to publishing the Fort Wayne newspaper.

For several months Nelson published the Fort Wayne *Sentinel*, laying down the law as he later did in Kansas City. "No single member of the council will be permitted to bulldoze the board of waterworks or to gratify his personal malice at the expense of the people—that might as well be understood now as hereafter," he wrote in one campaign. And when rumors circulated that the *Sentinel* wouldn't last long, Nelson turned sharply on his opponents. "The fossils of Columbia Street," he wrote, "continue to fume and rave and breathe forth dire predictions as to the *Sentinel*. They will be pleased to learn, no doubt, that the paper is in a thriving condition."

However, he soon decided to leave Fort Wayne, and to seek a larger and more progressive field for his publishing. He said he never had any doubt that he would succeed if he could keep his creditors from "sawing my legs off." One- and two-cent newspapers were building big circulations in Chicago, and Nelson prepared to enter that line of publishing. He had taken note of how the different railroad systems joined in Kansas City; and he selected that city for his next venture.

The driving force that operated in him was best indicated by Nelson himself, in a statement he made in later years. "I have never enjoyed being bossed, and I don't to this day," he said. "It was my disposition to think that no one had any rights over me."

He was thirty-nine years old and used to say that he had already made most of his mistakes when, on a foggy morning in 1880, he stepped from a train into Kansas City's cupolaed Union Depot, above which rose the giant West Bluff and the clifftop cluster of a city. He made his way, past the confidence men and town boomers who frequented the depot, past the rows of saloons that catered to the railroad and cattlemen, to the top of the city. The one name in Kansas City with which Nelson was familiar was that of Eugene Field, and Field was the first person he looked up. They walked together to the Marble Hall. The lanky poet had a habit of walking as though he were wading, bent forward a little. Nelson, of huge stature, was already portly. At the Marble Hall, Field introduced Nelson as the town's new publisher; and in accordance with custom he was issued a meal ticket on credit. Nelson often commented in later years, when he wished to indicate the degree of change in the times, that he had come to found a newspaper in a town where the leading restaurant was a saloon.

Eugene Field, melancholy poet with an elfish sense of humor, was in Kansas City only for the one year in which Nelson arrived; but during that time the poet greatly enriched the city's stock of legends. Born in St. Louis but brought up in New England, Field was almost a stranger to the state until he came out in 1870, at the age of twenty, to attend for a few months the University of Missouri. However, he always considered himself a true son of "poor old Mizzoorah." To use his own words, he was "on friendly terms with most of the native tribes, including the tree-dwellers of Callaway County, often shot by careless hunters who mistook them for possums or coons, and the amphibious mermaids of the Osage River, who came up every four years to vote the Democratic ticket."

Being the son of "rich yet honest" parents, Field had received an inheritance of something like twenty thousand dollars. Before he came to Kansas City, the money was entirely spent. As soon as he reached the age of twenty-one, he had set off with a friend for Europe, paying all expenses and writing and cabling frequently to his guardian for funds. At Florence, Italy, he was greeted by a cablegram to the effect that no more money was available. By selling and pawning his large stock of souvenirs, he was able to return to New York. There his guardian sent him a little money, enough for the trip to St. Louis. He worked for newspapers in St. Louis and St. Joseph, and in 1880 came to the Kansas City *Times*. He was the paper's managing editor, and he was paid a salary of twenty-nine dollars a week.

The poet was thirty years old, tall and cadaverous, with his pale skin stretched tightly over a big skull and his face perpetually solemn. He was already partly bald, and was letting his sideburns grow to preserve as much hair as possible. Before starting his day's work, he always rolled up his trouser legs, took down his suspenders and put on house slippers to give himself the maximum of ease and freedom. Then he propped his feet on the desk, sat on the end of his spine and wrote in his lap. This was the posture in which he wrote for the rest of his life.

When Field assumed his post in Kansas City, the Democratic *Times* and the Republican *Journal* were engaged in spirited rivalry. Each carried so much that was detracting or derogatory about the other that the newsboys sometimes called: "Here's your *Times*, all about the *Journal*; Here's your *Journal*, all about the *Times*." The poet fell in with the prevailing practice, and selected the *Journal's* well-known bent toward rigid economy as the target for his jibes. He claimed that all of the *Journal's* so-called special dispatches from Washington were shamelessly cribbed from the St. Louis, Cincinnati and Chicago papers. When the *Journal* retorted that its Washington correspondent was paid the adequate sum of five dollars a day, Field wrote: "Five dollars a day is a very paltry item in the *Times*; we pay more than that every week to the man who sprinkles our reporters' heels to keep them from catching fire as they fly around for news."

D. K. Abeel, business manager of the *Journal*, did not consider himself parsimonious; and the jibes stirred him to a reprisal against Field's employer, a lanky and ascetic publisher named Dr. Morrison Munford. Dr. Munford's desk was placed in front of a large window in such a way as to give somewhat the impression of his being on display in a glass cage—an impression heightened by the publisher's invariable habit of wearing formal clothes in his office. The offices of the two newspapers were across the street from each other. One day after glaring across the street, Abeel wrote and sent to the composing room the following paragraph:

"It is long and thin and has a hungry look; it is kept in a glass cage. What is it?"

The paragraph kept recurring without explanation or comment in odd corners of the *Journal*. Those who knew the story of its origin used to say that this was the only paragraph the business manager ever bothered to write for the paper, and that he only made one change. After Dr. Munford had moved his desk, the paragraph read: "It is long and thin and has a hungry look; it used to be kept in a glass cage. What is it?"

Kansas City's most famous Eugene Field story concerned his friendship with George Gaston, who eventually acquired the honorary title of "colonel" and retired in some wealth to the rolling acres of a farm which today is part of the campus of the University of Kansas City. In his earlier years, Colonel Gaston was the keeper of a downtown bar on Sixth Street between Delaware and Wyandotte. Although Field was a light drinker, and in his later years did not drink at all, he was fond of companionship and with other newspapermen frequented this bar. Since he was never able to keep the slightest account of his finances, he not only failed to pay his bill at

Gaston's but at times inveigled the barkeeper into various expenses in his behalf.

One evening Gaston was counting his day's receipts, and sighed with satisfaction: "Ah! One hundred and ten dollars." "Well, George," said Field, "don't you think you could afford to set up the oysters on that?" Gaston was by no means a spendthrift, and the suggestion slightly dampened his spirit; but he agreed. They went to the Marble Hall for the oysters. When they were seated at a table, Field suggested that they should also have some wine. "Now look here, Gene, I'm paying for the dinner, but if you want any wine you'll have to buy it yourself." Field then produced two large bottles of champagne, Gaston's own, which the poet had managed to lift from a shelf and conceal under his coat before leaving the bar.

Gaston appeared to be getting the worst of the relationship; yet when Field stopped coming to his place, Gaston was alarmed. Field had run up a bill of one hundred and thirty-seven dollars, and was embarrassed to appear until he could pay. His absence did not at all suit Gaston, because the poet, widely celebrated in the town for his wit and humor as well as for his verse,* was the type of person to whom legends attached, and around whom a crowd always gathered. Apart from friendship, he was valuable for attracting business to the place.

So Gaston sent word to Field that he wanted to see him. When Field appeared he asked him if he had a dime. The poet fumbled in his pocket and brought forth ten cents; whereupon

---

* Of Field's Kansas City poems, the only one to become well known was "The Little Peach." It appeared in the Kansas City *Times* in August of 1880 and began:

> A little peach in the orchard grew—
> A little peach of emerald hue;
> Warmed by the sun and wet by the dew,
> It grew.

Gaston, to place everything on the former footing, handed him his bill, marked "paid in full." Much of the effectiveness of Eugene Field's humor resulted from the fact that he always appeared to be completely serious. On this occasion he stood solemnly for several moments, looking at the receipted bill and not saying anything. Then he glanced inquiringly up and down the line at the bar, turned back to Gaston and said severely: "George, isn't it customary for the bartender to set 'em up when a man pays his bill?"

Toward the end of 1880, a printer arrived from the Denver *Republican*, with authority to offer Eugene Field more money to work out there. The printer went to the *Times* office, and found Field in his usual office attire. As soon as "more money" was mentioned, Field took off his house slippers, looked at them mournfully for a few moments and threw them in the waste basket. He pulled up his suspenders and began to prepare himself for the street. Receiving no answer and not being familiar with the poet's office rituals, the printer presently asked: "What are you going to do? What shall I tell them?" Field inclined his head toward the waste basket containing the house slippers: "Can't you see I'm already resigning?"

After Field went to Denver, Nelson made most of Kansas City's journalistic history. His *Star* announced itself in September of 1880 as "a first-class cheap afternoon newspaper." It promised to be "a paper for the people—independent, enterprising, spicy, readable, truthful and entertaining," and said it would furnish "news of fires before the smoke has cleared, of murders before the body of the victim is cold in death, and of weddings before the happy bride can collect her senses."

Behind the *Star* sat Nelson, a tremendous man, weighing nearly three hundred pounds in his later years. Because he was short-legged, he appeared even larger when he was sitting down, looming behind a desk with what William Allen White described as "a general Himalayan effect"; and he had a deep bass voice which came out in cavernous booms and rumblings. This massive figure, this giant, bullfroglike man, whose most frequent expression was an explosive "By God!" became the best known of the men who were thrown to the top of the heap in the scramble that accompanied Kansas City's rapid organization.

The "cheap paper" at first was thought of as a separate field of publishing, rather than as one which would displace the five-cent dailies. Pennies had never had much circulation; and Nelson was obliged to import several barrels of them before his paper, priced at two cents, could sell. Most of the *Star's* early announcements were devoted to arguing that there was room for an additional paper of this type—the size of which, it was stated, would never be more than four pages. However, the success of the *Star* was so immediate that at the end of three months it boasted the largest circulation in town.

Then came the real-estate boom, during which the *Star* was the only Kansas City newspaper to get itself on a firm financial footing. Nelson held to a policy sometimes phrased as "Boom not, that ye be not busted." The publisher probably would have been inclined to speculate in real estate; but he had a shrewd business manager, August F. Seested, who held him in check. Seested several times threatened to resign when Nelson was prepared to embark on speculative ventures. Consequently, except for some rather extensive property acquired as his scale of living rose, Nelson's only business interest was in the *Star*—which proved to be ample.

During the flush years of the boom, it was easy to sell real-estate advertising by the column and page. But Nelson and Seested concentrated on signing the infant department stores on annual, self-renewing contracts, with "keep alive" clauses requiring some advertisement every day. The stores grew and flourished, the *Star* was established as their principal advertising medium, and the paper thus had an enduring source of revenue when the bottom dropped out of real-estate values. Although other papers continued to publish for fifty years, it is scarcely an exaggeration to say that after the boom in the eighties no newspaper except the *Star* consistently made money in Kansas City.

Such was the prestige of the paper that Nelson was often in a position to dictate to his advertisers. One year when the *Star* raised its advertising rates, the manager of the leading theater tried to revolt, and withdrew his advertising. The theater manager soon found he was losing business and decided he would pay the increased rate after all, but the *Star* would not again accept his advertising at any price. Nelson sat back with great satisfaction to watch the theater's patronage decline. A committee of businessmen came to the newspaper office to plead for the theater manager's financial life. Nelson merely said he thought it better that the man did not have any more financial life. The theater's advertising did not appear in the *Star* for three or four years. It was once suggested to Nelson that he should forgive his enemies, to which he promptly replied: "Humph! *You* can forgive my enemies; I'll forgive *yours.*"

The *Star* was a crusading newspaper, and no one was immune from Nelson's campaigning. He first campaigned against the nation-wide telegraph monopoly organized by Jay Gould. Gould was sufficiently disturbed to ban telegrams to the *Star* for a time in 1881. Colonel Kersey Coates of Quality Hill was still the leader of the Northern commercial element at the time of Nelson's arrival, and Nelson selected Colonel Coates as his next target. He declared in the *Star* that the storied Coates Opera House was a "firetrap." Colonel Coates was highly incensed, and said something pointed about blackmail, but later did make the necessary repairs in his Opera House.

Although Frank James never received the appointment, some years after his surrender to the governor, it was proposed to make him chief doorkeeper at a session of the Missouri legislature. James was seeking the post, and the *Star* sought public reaction to the possible appointment. Although there was opposition to it, no unfavorable comment could be obtained. As the *Star* reported: " 'I can't afford to say a word; I have to make a living here and I can't afford to antagonize that part of the population which sympathizes with the Southern cause,' was the general remark."

Nelson, however, commented at length in his newspaper. "It is daily urged in Missouri that we let bygones be bygones," he said, "and that we should not revive the passions of the war, and that we should admit that every man fought for what he believed to be right." But he added that the activities of the James boys had given the whole country the impression that Missouri favored lawlessness, and then spoke sardonically of the "fine publicity" which would come to the state if outlawry were rewarded by a legislative appointment. He also wryly raised the question as to whether James would need his six-shooters in the work.

Nelson campaigned for bridges, viaducts and bicycle paths, and against franchises, "dripping dirt wagons" and sore-shouldered dray horses; for policing streetcars, flood protection and smoke control, and against lotteries, loan sharks and fee grabbers; for tree planting, preservation of birds, and windows in the farm woman's kitchen, and against "encroaching pushcarts," "snitch" lawyers and quack doctors. His paper was sometimes called "The Daily William Rockhill Nelson." Once when he was campaigning for "dollar gas," someone approached him and said: "But surely, colonel, you want to be fair to the company." "Fair to the company!" he replied.

"By God, that's what I *don't* want to be. When has the company been fair to the city?"

Of all the "benighted non-comprehension" against which Nelson labored, the worst by his own account was that which greeted his campaign for public parks. People wanted to know what was the use of parks when half the town consisted of vacant lots. In this connection, Nelson invented The Hammer and Padlock Club, which supposedly consisted of people who went about with hammers under their coats to beat the life out of civic projects, and with padlocks on their pocketbooks to prevent raising the necessary taxes. In 1897, the issue was the "West and North Terracing Ordinance." One day on the front page of the *Star* appeared a drawing of "The President of the Hammer and Padlock Club," represented as a shriveled, dried-up, old man, a regular Father Time, except for one bulging arm muscle for the wielding of his hammer. And from the top of the page ran the following:

KNOCK! KNOCK! KNOCK!

Session of the Hammer
and Padlock Club
Last Night.

The Old Gilliss Hotel Resounds
With Wails Against Parks—
Anarchy in Demand for
Improvement!—The
Sacred Rights of
Vacant Lot
Owners.

NOTE: The hammers forgotten in
the meeting may be obtained from
the property man at police headquarters, where they have been
deposited.

The culminating sensation of the park controversy occurred when the Taxkickers' League met last night at the Gilliss Hotel to consider further steps in the campaign against parks.

"Suppose we are finally forced to pay for these parks?" was the question which precipitated the storm.

"I'll go to jail first," screamed a woman.

"If all legal means fail," shouted a man, "then we are face to face with anarchy!"

"The small property owners are not complaining, because they can take advantage of the twenty years' payments and won't feel it," said another. "But we have too much ready money to pay interest. And the thing is a cold-blooded plot against the sacred rights of unimproved property. Make us pay interest? Ask millionaires to pay interest? Aha!"

"Gentlemen, I think we can call a spade. We are facing a new issue, namely the rabble. The improvidents, spendthrifts, the idle laborers voted for the parks. It was a revolution against thrift! (Applause)

"Youths who, many of them, have three suits of clothes; men who buy cut roses at seventy-five cents a dozen for a lady friend, and spend $1 on a meal—yes, as much as $1.50 and even $2 on a single meal—they voted for parks. They want to see the money flow; they want to re-enact the folly of the boom, when laboring men smoked cigars and every fool had money and spent it.

"What right have people who don't pay taxes, who own no land, who wish to enjoy the music but don't pay the fiddler, to vote these enormous parks on men who scrimped when others spent their money broadcast? During what may justly be called a fool's paradise, I saved and bought land . . . I am being sliced. . . . They will want us to build theaters next! . . . It is a plot; a p-l-o-t. . . . And I am just enough of a knocker who goes about with a padlock on my pocketbook and a hammer under my coat to pay my share toward getting a law that only property owners may vote. (Great applause)

"I move that the subscription be taken up now," roared
the same voice.

But a dozen voices called out for adjournment at once,
and the crowd poured out so hastily that several hammers
were left behind.

Nelson's opponents also received such designations as
"Colonel Pullback" and "Judge Goodenough Fermee." "Could
the heckler and the mossback have had his way about it,"
Nelson later said, "Kansas City would still be a straggling,
ill-conditioned river town, perched on dizzy bluffs and hiding
in precipitous hollows, with a wheezy old ferry boat paddling
across the river to the rival town of Harlem. The tax rate
would have been low, and Kansas City would have been
flat. Not a desirable feature, not a fine street, not a public
building exceeding the cost and appearance of an old-
fashioned courthouse would exist in Kansas City if the protests of the kickers and the gentlemen with hammers under
their coats had been effectual."

One of those to feel the pressure of Nelson's campaigning,
in two ways, was Colonel Thomas H. Swope. Swope had
owned the land which became the center of the business
district, and was considered the town's richest man. Until
he reached the age of seventy, he had lived a rather parsimonious existence, but under the pressure of Nelson's
campaigning he was induced to donate 1,331 acres for a
public park, known as Swope Park, which became one of
the main features of Kansas City. By means of more campaigning in his newspaper, Nelson produced for the dedication of the park a crowd of eighteen thousand people; and
for a time Colonel Swope was the outstanding public citizen
featured in the *Star*.

Colonel Swope's status changed a year later because of a
downtown lot which he owned, and which was just across the

street from the *Star's* office. Some excavation had been
started for building on the lot, but the project had been
abandoned. A pond had formed in the bottom of the excavation, after which the outer edges were given over to
billboards. Every time the mountainous Mr. Nelson swiveled
around in his chair, his eye fell on this eyesore which was
just across the street, and for which Colonel Swope was responsible.

One day the *Star* appeared with a front page drawing titled
"Colonel Swope's Exhortation to the Tax Kickers." Swope was
shown speaking from a raft in the middle of the vacant lot's
pond, while his audience of fellow millionaires was perched
elf-like on top of the billboards. And Colonel Swope was
saying: "Fellow property owners, oppressed millionaires and
members of the Taxkickers' league. . . . I am inspired to
fresh courage by standing here in the last ditch which I
bought for $150 a front foot. It is now worth $1,500 a foot.
I wouldn't sell it for $2,000! (Cheers). . . . See to the pad-
locks on your pocketbooks and grasp your hammers more
firmly. . . . Let us stand forever in one place like we have
always stood and refuse to move one jot or tittle, one iota
or one cent."

Colonel Swope was a Kentuckian of usually mild demeanor,
but he was highly insulted by this drawing. He stalked into
the *Star's* office, collared the first employee he encountered,
and in a shaking voice said: "Young man, you tell your boss
that if my name *ever* appears in the *Star* again, I will kill him."
With that, Colonel Swope turned on his heel and walked
out. "By golly," commented Nelson, "I think he means it."

In addition to being outspoken, the *Star* early acquired a
reputation for the high quality of its reading matter. Nelson
reprinted a great many articles from eastern papers and from
magazines. He considered these reprints, more than any

other feature, responsible for the success of the paper, and he leased a private wire to New York to speed the delivery of them. The news men sometimes were irritated by the fact that timely news from the East had to reach them as best it could on commercial telegraph wires, while a private wire was bringing in Nelson's reprints. But the publisher often preferred to place a magazine article or a letter from a reader at the top of the front page. Nelson also distributed sections of the classics through his paper. Across from a headline reading "POLICE DENSELY IGNORANT—KNEW OF GAMBLING ONLY THROUGH NEWSPAPERS," might be "DEATH OF THE LAST MOHICAN," "HOW TOM SAWYER GOT THE FENCE WHITEWASHED," "THE DEFENSE OF SOCRATES," or one of Emerson's essays.

Although it drew from the best in literature, the *Star* seldom contained anything that was difficult to read. Nelson hated high-sounding phraseology. He was attracted both to the lectures of Robert Ingersoll and the sermons of Billy Sunday because they used the vernacular; "got down where people live," as Nelson put it. When Kansas City opened its first art gallery, a *Star* reporter wrote an article describing the exquisite appearance of the hall and the paintings, using the word "exquisite" six or eight times. Nelson made no objection to the article, but he had the reporter insert in one place: "Many persons frankly confess they are Indians so far as the great 'Madonna pictures' are concerned," and in another, the overheard remark: "Well, this ought to rub some of the lard off of Kansas City." Even in dealing with the classics, Nelson sometimes had the subject matter converted into the vernacular. An article in the *Star* headed "PYTHAGORAS—WHO BACKED HIS PHILOSOPHY WITH HIS FISTS," referred to the venerable Greek as "one of the heavy artillery of the philosophy business." One of a series of articles called "THE CLASSICS BY

WIRE" was datelined "Rome, July 10, 64 A.D.—(Special Dispatch)—" and bore this head: "FIRE DESTROYS ROME—EARLY MORNING BLAZE THOUGHT TO HAVE BEEN OF INCENDIARY ORIGIN —DID NERO DO IT?" "The public," said Nelson, "does not yearn to have its opinion guided or instructed. It wants to get the news and be entertained. If we can sneak up behind a man when he isn't looking and instruct him, all well and good; but if he gets the idea that our main purpose is to edify him, he runs so fast we never can catch him."

Nelson published a highly competent, readable, vigorous and honest newspaper. Many good men were glad to work for him for that reason—to the extent, almost, of contributing their services. For although he took a large view in public matters, Nelson could sometimes be close-fisted in his own affairs. He believed in the eight-hour day and higher wages— "I have no fear that the operators will be unable to take care of themselves; I'm interested in the man who digs the coal," he said—but he could think of a great many reasons for not increasing a wage in his own plant. "Any man worth more than $5,000 a year would be in business for himself," he would say. That was his reason for not increasing the salaries of his top executives. As for members of the general staff, he frequently said: "The surest way to ruin a good newspaperman is to put some money in his pocket." This was a deep-seated conviction with him, and he repeated it often enough to discourage the boldest reporter from asking for a raise.

There were other newspaper publishers holding such views, as was learned by A. B. Macdonald, one of the best reporters produced by the *Star*. When Macdonald was seventy years old and had covered two-thirds of the city's history, he was awarded a Pulitzer prize for reporting. In those later years, he was well known to the *Star's* readers in four states. But at this time he was a young reporter. At the *Star* he had tried repeatedly for an increase in pay, with no success. Then the doors of opportunity seemed to open. Macdonald came to the attention of Frederick G. Bonfils, who offered him a job on the paper which Bonfils was just then building toward prominence—the Denver *Post*.

Bonfils, who by contrast with Nelson was dapper, athletic and black-mustached, had made his original fortune in gambling, and in Kansas City. Although the antigambling law of 1881 had permanently ended the reign of King Faro, gambling in various other forms soon returned. There were big poker and dice games, and cock fights in wooded arenas where the cattlemen sometimes peeled off several thousand dollars for a single bet. Lotteries were especially popular, and Bonfils had been the head of an organization which handled one of the most successful—the Little Louisiana Lottery. According to information given the *Star*, Bonfils increased his lottery profits by refusing to pay off on the winning tickets.

One of his victims was Maurice Barrymore, who was in Kansas City for an engagement at the Coates Opera House. The actor bought a "Little Louisiana" ticket which won twenty dollars. He sent a man to get the money, and the man returned saying he could not collect. Barrymore himself went to the office of Frederick G. Bonfils. "We don't pay those things, except once in a while for the sake of the publicity," Bonfils told him. He then became almost jovial, and placed a hand on Barrymore's shoulder. "Your ticket is no good, no good at all; just throw it away," he advised. Barrymore shook the hand off roughly, and offered to fight, but Bonfils waved him aside: "You have your way of doing business, and I have mine."

Such was the story that, one day in 1893, the amazed and

angered Barrymore told to the *Star*. Nelson then campaigned against the Little Louisiana Lottery so vigorously that Bonfils was obliged to leave town, taking with him a large part of the million and a half dollars his lottery business had grossed. Bonfils decided that the newspaper business was better than the Little Louisiana Lottery. He bought the Denver *Post*, and there copied the idea which Nelson had so forcefully called to his attention. In Denver, Bonfils also campaigned against lotteries. Once the Denver *Post* was well established as that city's leading newspaper, he laid plans to return to Kansas City and square accounts with his publishing enemy. As a part of his plan, he looked over Nelson's staff and decided to take A. B. Macdonald.

"You're wasting your time in Kansas City; come on out to Denver and you'll make twice as much money," he told Macdonald.

Double what he was getting sounded good to Macdonald, so he went to Denver and worked one week. At the end of the week, he received the same twenty-five dollars he had been drawing in Kansas City. "You said if I came out here I'd make twice as much money," Macdonald protested to Bonfils. "Oh yes," said the publisher, "and you will, my boy, you will. But of course I meant after you had learned the town; you can't expect to make it right away."

Pending the determination of his salary in Denver, Macdonald had not resigned from the *Star*. He had only taken his vacation. So he freely expressed his opinion of the Denver publisher, and then returned to the Kansas City *Star*.

Sometime afterward Bonfils, with his partner Harry Tammen, began publishing the Kansas City *Post*, an afternoon newspaper competing with the *Star*. Tammen was a former bartender, a short, round and generous man who gave away fifty dollars a day in tips and smoked fifty-cent cigars. (He claimed that Bonfils often stood close to him to inhale free smoke from these cigars.) But the one partner's generosity did the newspapermen no good, because Bonfils kept the books and determined the salaries. He still wanted A. B. Macdonald and called Macdonald to his office.

"What you said out in Denver is all forgotten," Bonfils assured him. "I want you to be city editor of the Kansas City *Post*, and I'm willing to pay you sixty-five dollars a week."

"Maybe we had better have a contract," suggested Macdonald.

"Certainly; you write it out; write anything you want."

Macdonald wrote what appeared to be an extemporaneous note, and Bonfils signed it. Macdonald thus became city editor of the Kansas City *Post*. However, there is nothing very permanent about a job on a newly booming newspaper. Macdonald was soon out as city editor, and Bonfils was trying to cut him back to reporter's pay. "My contract," reminded Macdonald. "That," said Bonfils, "was if you were city editor."

Once again Macdonald had taken a precaution. Before going to Bonfils' office, he had stopped at a law office and had memorized a legal form. What had appeared to be an extemporaneous note was an iron-bound contract. Bonfils finally was convinced of this. Macdonald drew sixty-five dollars a week for the rest of his contract year, and then returned to the *Star* with a reputation as the only man ever to get the best of the Denver publisher. Bonfils and Tammen published the Kansas City *Post* for thirteen years, matching red headlines against the *Star's* conservative makeup; but the *Star* always continued to receive the heavy volume of advertising.

To people in Kansas City, Bonfils and Tammen were incredible. They were a completely unmatched pair, who had somehow formed an enduring partnership. At the time Bonfils was trying to cut him back to reporter's pay, Macdonald was as interested in trying to fathom the man as he was in the money. He almost pleaded with the publisher to explain himself. "Mr. Bonfils," he said, "I can't understand it. I know you like my work; you let me handle your money; you trust me; I I know you like me, and you know I like you. In fact, we're good friends. And yet here it is, a difference of a few hundred dollars, which doesn't mean a thing to you and means a great deal to me, and you are trying to beat me out of it. Mr. Bonfils, I want to know, why would you do such a thing to me?"

Mr. Bonfils devoted some moments of what appeared to be serious thought to the question, and found no ready solution. "I guess," he said, "that it's just a matter of principle."

So A. B. Macdonald, the great reporter, worked through his best reporting years for twenty-five or thirty-five dollars a week. At thirty-five dollars a week, he was one of Nelson's higher-paid employees. His methods were far different than those usually attributed to newspapermen. When he arrived for an interview, he would announce: "I'm A. B. Macdonald of the *Star*, and I've come to tell *your* side of the story." Then he sat down immediately in front of his subject, produced a thick pad of paper, and proceeded at a furious rate to take down in longhand every word that was said. For years after typewriters came into general use, Nelson would not have them in the *Star*. He said they would "make writing too mechanical," or "interrupt the flow of thought." But Macdonald never needed a typewriter, as he wrote so rapidly in longhand that a good telegraph operator could not keep up with him. If he got a little behind in taking down an interview, he would say, "Just a minute, this is *very* important," while bending over his pad to catch up.

When he returned to the office, Macdonald would turn

out a story in the plainest of words, almost as they had come to him. There was the case of the poor widow living in a shack on the Sandtown Flats. "I found her on Thanksgiving day," wrote Macdonald. "She and her children were without food and shivering with cold; the wind was whistling through the cracks in the shack. 'But fresh air is good,' she told me. 'The children are cold, but they are healthy.' She was dressing one child in its rags. 'Too much clothing isn't good for little ones,' she said. They had eaten nothing but potatoes for days. 'It's good food,' she assured me."

Those lines made the Sandtown widow the richest woman in her neighborhood. More baskets of food, coal and clothing were sent than her shack would contain. Other pieces by Macdonald were equally effective. Despite his success, he was the object of much good-humored derision from his fellow workers, who said he believed everything he was told and chuckled over his use of homespun detail not ordinarily dignified by inclusion in the columns of the press. But Macdonald stuck to his own methods. "Why was Dickens great?" he would argue. "Dickens was a simple writer; he didn't even write correctly, according to the rules. But he wrote about everyday things that are close to the lives of people—he was a good reporter."

Such reporting was favored by Nelson, who presented some strange contrasts. Nelson's favorite photograph of himself was a grim pose with his eyes narrowed and his arms folded across his chest—a Captain Kidd in an indignant moment. Because of his unusual bulk, he seldom appeared among the people of the city and the grim pose of the portrait represented the way he was known to the general public. On the other hand, he had a practice of importing squirrels of different types to release in the parks, and of stopping on his way home to feed them; a rather bizarre hobby for a man of his size. He had a real liking for his valet Ben—"Wait, don't tell that now; wait till Ben gets here, he'll enjoy that," he would say—and he was over-fond of his only child Laura, whose marriage he vigorously, and even desperately, opposed. When she married anyhow, the publisher's note with his wedding gift read humbly: "Here I am again with a miserable draft . . . My only explanation is that I can't help it . . . You'll forgive me I know."

In the late eighties when his income from advertising was swelling, Nelson looked around for a place to live. Quality Hill was deteriorating, being too close to the business district. Nelson selected several hundred acres much farther south, and built a rambling, baronial home, seated so far back from the street that an eighteen-hole golf course might have been laid out on his front lawn.

He also built one hundred other houses in the Rockhill District. He never gave leases on these houses, because he wanted to be able to oust any of his tenants who incurred his displeasure. Like his father, he prided himself on broad democratic principles; but the style of his living assumed a feudal aspect. For that reason, he was called "The Baron of Brush Creek"—the creek meandered through his property. His father visited him there in 1890, and found his problem boy already the most powerful man in the new Kansas City.

Nelson was an extremely difficult man to characterize. He was a modern Peter the Great—a humanitarian, a progressive, certainly, but with strong tendencies toward iron-handed rule. "I have tried being gentle," he once said, "but I never did well in my stocking feet." He was known as a "Baron," but he was a publisher with the common touch. He had hundreds of personal prejudices, and yet in the fields of larger thought he had an independence of mind that lifted him above usual patterns of thinking. His strong purposes, and strong and highly individual traits of character, made him important to Kansas City; and, when the influence of his paper had spread over four states, made him important also on the national scene. His last great battle was for the Progressive party and Theodore Roosevelt in 1912.

CHAPTER ELEVEN

A Capable Man

THE STORY OF THE PENDERGAST political reign, which continued in Kansas City for more than half a century, begins with the old Union Depot in the West Bottoms. This station was only two years old in 1880 when James Pendergast arrived, but a considerable business district was developing around it. There was a row of twenty-three saloons on the block-long Union Avenue which led to the station, and near by were the factories, the railroad shops and cattle yards, the boarding houses and hotels.

For two years James Pendergast worked as an iron puddler at the Jarboe Iron Works. Then in 1882, he opened a boarding house called The American Inn, and a saloon which was around the corner from the depot. He was a big man who wore a big mustache and a derby hat. He never forgot a man's face, his name or his problem; he was always ready with advice and help; and he had a force of character and decision that won respect. Like Eugene Field's Casey, he ran a "tabble dote." The food at his place was excellent, and he himself was a genial and hearty host—a man you had to like. He became a great favorite with the railroad men.

His plunge into politics came more or less accidentally in 1884. He suggested to his customers and acquaintances that they vote for Leander J. Talbott for mayor. There was nothing unusual about the suggestion, but the result was impressive. Talbott carried the first ward by 144 votes, whereas the Democratic alderman carried it by only ten. The difference between their pluralities was plainly due to the number and loyalty of James Pendergast's friends. Thereafter he was "King of the First." No matter how far out in the south part of town a candidate might live, it behooved him to come down to the bottom lands and see James Pendergast if he expected to carry the first ward.

The West Bottoms were being industrialized. One year there might be five thousand voters in a precinct, and a few years later there would be none—the entire area having been covered with industrial plants. The population was being pushed out of the Kansas River bottoms onto the top of the bluff to occupy Colonel Coates' Quality Hill, also into the old levee district where the steamboats once had discharged freight and passengers bound for the Great West, and into a little more distant section that was included in the North End. James Pendergast followed the trend by opening a second saloon on North Main Street, in the old levee district. After he opened his second saloon he controlled the votes of both the first and second wards, or about twenty per cent of the city's vote.

In 1892, James Pendergast was elected to the city council. He thereafter served for eighteen years as a city alderman. As old-timers remember him during those years, his hand was always in his pocket. "Here," he would say to a needy-looking customer in one of his saloons, "take fifty cents; spend it somewhere else." His second saloon was near the City Hall, and he cashed many pay checks for city employees. If a man needed a short-term loan, he could get it from James Pendergast, without interest. Or, if a family were reported in need, James Pendergast would arrange to send out baskets of food and sacks of coal. If flood waters crept over the bottom lands, he put on hip boots and helped rescue the possessions of his constituents. His charity was in the nature of a blank check, since a number of his friends had instructions to help anyone they found in need, and send the bill to him.

The old levee district and near-by bottom lands became the home of the poorest. A survey in this area once showed four hundred "un-churched" blocks. There were mission houses, but not money enough to support churches after the well-to-do people moved to the south part of town. Another survey showed that in one block 2,000 men lived with no other home than a room or a part of a room. In Kansas City, these men were called "gandy dancers." The name originally applied to seasonal railroad workers, from their appearance as they jumped up and down on an iron bar to loosen a rail; but it was later used to refer to any derelict, or any man temporarily down on his luck. In good weather, the "gandy dancers" could be seen sitting like flocks of weary birds on curbs and in doorways along North Main Street.

These were the forgotten men—forgotten, that is, by everyone except the politicians. It could be said of the Pendergasts as was sometimes said of the bosses of Tammany Hall: "They got rich by helping the poor." Bordering the "flop house" district were low-rent sections where James Pendergast's charity was also appreciated, and rooming-house districts for the railroad and cattlemen, who never forgot him. Bordering too was the business district, the concentration area for the saloons which he represented, and the operating base for the Metropolitan Street Railway Company and other interests with which he was allied. It all made one unified, downtown domain which James Pendergast ruled with a somewhat weary hand.

This was the area in which the Pendergasts' "reign" continued for more than fifty years. They might lose an election, even be crushingly defeated, but they always carried the river wards, or downtown wards, and they always had this solid, dependable voting strength with which to stage a comeback in the next election. A visitor at one of the mission houses in the bottom lands could scarcely expect to find more than one or two anti-Pendergast voters in a hundred. The same situation made vote-padding and ghost-voting extremely easy, since the Republican election judges at some of the polling places were mere straw men, pushed around by the overwhelming majority.

That he was a saloonkeeper added to, rather than subtracted from, James Pendergast's influence. For at that time, especially in the levee district, the saloon was the place where a man was most likely to go for advice and help. Charley Nelson, one of Kansas City's old-time barkeepers, once publicly offered to bet five hundred dollars that he could show more charity in a saloon than could be shown in any church. Possibly he could have won the wager, since, like Pendergast, most of the saloonkeepers were politicians and were receiving a return in votes for the bread they cast upon the waters. But there were no takers for Charley Nelson's wager, a fact concerning which he frequently expressed regret throughout his life.

With all his spending, James Pendergast prospered in a business way. Taxes on liquor were not what they later became, and saloon-keeping was profitable. The *Star* once listed James Pendergast's assets as follows: "A farm in Kansas; a farm near Lamar, Missouri; blooded stock, horses, cattle, swine and sheep; several pieces of real estate in the most desirable parts of the city; interest in several paying businesses; fine clothes and expensive jewelry; and, last but not least, legions of friends." Apart from his own resources, he had access to a wide variety of "campaign contributions," as the politicians of the day were not hesitant about bargaining for funds. Once when the *Star* was campaigning for an amendment to the city charter, a politician approached William Rockhill Nelson and said: "Colonel, you seem to want this amendment pretty badly, and you can have it. But it'll take a little money for the workers." The amendment was essential to the system of parks and boulevards which was Nelson's favorite project, and he didn't mind conceding afterward that he had "made the necessary arrangements."

At the time James Pendergast rose in politics, there were ten city wards, and the number was later increased to fourteen. He himself controlled the first and second wards, and one of his brothers, Mike, controlled the tenth. The only political boss to keep pace with the Pendergasts was Joseph Shannon of the ninth ward. Shannon was a lawyer, in appearance somewhat resembling President Harding, and he had a great reputation for learning and shrewdness. There were other ward bosses, but James Pendergast and Joseph Shannon rose so much above them that the others allied themselves with one of these two. The factional fighting between the Pendergast and Shannon followings then became legendary.

One year in the nineties a political writer said that the Pendergast crowd had "voted everything in sight, including the goats on the hillsides," and that faction became known as the Pendergast Goats. Another writer wrote that the

Shannon men had "flocked to the polls like scared rabbits after hunters had beaten the brush," and they became the Shannon Rabbits. On occasions when the Republicans did manage to get into office, it was commonly said that they had succeeded only because these two Democratic factions, the Pendergast Goats and the Shannon Rabbits, could not get together long enough to vote the same ticket on election day.

In general it was the tradition that the Pendergast Goats moved ahead by main strength and numbers, whereas the Rabbits were expected to "live by their wits." It was said that all the Goat meetings were held in first-floor halls, so that if anyone was thrown out a window he wouldn't be hurt much. C. S. Demaree, an old resident, used to tell how he came to Kansas City in the early days and, wishing to enter politics, aligned himself with the Shannon Rabbits. He was sent, all unsuspecting, to a meeting of the Goats who were being addressed by the mayor. He was told to rise at a certain point and say: "Mr. Mayor, will you please tell this audience how much money you received from the Home Telephone Company?" He did so, touching a sore point, as there had recently been a telephone merger which had caused much criticism. Demaree never was sure what hit him, but he suddenly landed in the street. "I emerged from that meeting a statesman," he used to say. He thereafter kept within the tradition.

The fighting between the factions enabled the Republicans to hold the city administrations during most of the nineties. Then in 1900 James Pendergast backed a winning ticket, headed by James A. Reed for mayor. James A. Reed was an extraordinary public speaker, who contributed a considerable part of the color to the Pendergast era in Kansas City's history. At the time he ran for mayor in 1900, he had just completed a term as public prosecutor, during which he had obtained 285 convictions in 287 prosecutions; and he had already developed the oratorical prowess which made him a nationally known figure when he reached the United States Senate. Between James Pendergast's acumen and Reed's oratory, the ticket won handily, and Pendergast men went into jobs. Brother Tom Pendergast—of whom more was heard later—was given the post of street commissioner at $2,000 a year.

During the remaining ten years he lived, James Pendergast was the chief political weight in Kansas City. He controlled the city council on almost every issue. To the end, he remained the saloonkeeper interested in any man's problem, and the custodian of a seemingly limitless bank account for aid to the poor. Besides dealing in jobs, political favors, and charitable activities, he placed himself on the progressive side of most issues. "You can't stop progress," he would say, sometimes sighing as though he might like to do it if he could. When the direct primary came to displace the so-called "mob primary" which his strong men had so often controlled, he surprised his followers by favoring the direct vote. And, although the *Star* feuded with Mayor Reed, Pendergast supported many of Nelson's city-building projects.

Despite his substantial political rise, James Pendergast always seemed a little surprised to learn from reading the newspapers that he wielded so much power. As far as he was concerned, the situation was essentially the same as it was at the beginning, when as proprietor of The American Inn he had asked his friends to vote for a candidate for mayor. "That's all there is to this 'boss' business—friends," he said. "You can't coerce people into doing things for you; you can't make 'em vote for you. I never coerced anybody in my life. Whenever you see a man bulldozing anybody, he don't last long. Still, I've been called a boss. All there is to it is having friends, doing things for people and then later they'll do things for you."

The politician's creed in James Pendergast's era was rigid in some respects, and loose in others. The keeping of promises was essential to the operation of a political machine, where most of the agreements were oral, and this virtue was greatly exalted. The Pendergasts never failed to keep a promise, and even went out of their way to keep promises which had become outdated and might well have been allowed to lapse. Likewise, since political operations were based on the exchange of favors, ingratitude was the worst evil. The Rabbit and Goat factions might have difficulty in getting together on a candidate, but they could close ranks instantly for the purpose of chastising a man guilty of the cardinal sin of failing to appreciate and return a favor.

Such stress was placed on these political virtues that they threatened to exclude all others. Once a man who had been operating a "Novelty Theater," where short-skirted and pantyless girls sold beer and wine at fancy prices, was forced to leave town. There had been one murder, several shootings and innumerable swindles in his establishment. "He has sold his last three cents' worth of beer for a dollar and closed up," said the *Star*. The *Star* then suggested that perhaps in a politician's eyes this man was not a bad fellow, since "in the language of the day, he 'stood by his word, stuck by his friends and was game.'" To the politicians, "as good as his word" was enough recommendation for any man.

No such regard was felt for sterling virtue which might stand in the way of winning elections. On the contrary, it was expected that a politician would seize upon every advantage. James Pendergast often reminded his followers

"You can't saw wood with a hammer." Once when there were charges that the police controlled the polling places, his candidate for mayor, W. T. Kemper, resigned as police commissioner, thus giving up control of the force. Pendergast suspected that the police did have a good deal to do with the outcome of elections, and concluded that his candidate had been receiving bad advice from perfidious friends. "They've buncoed him," mourned Pendergast. "They've taken away his gun; disarmed him out on the prairie. Who buncoed my friend W. T. Kemper?" As though to confirm Pendergast's forebodings, Kemper subsequently was defeated. In general, a candidate who did not take advantage of every means which favored his side was viewed by James Pendergast as a foolish and misguided man.

Something of this philosophy was expressed in the ritual with which Brother Tom Pendergast bought his daily newspaper. Brother Tom—sixteen years younger than James— was a fine figure of a man, wearing a mustache, bowler hat, three-inch collar and black coat. He would ease down the street with the slight sidle peculiar to muscular men, would receive his newspaper, and would drop a coin into the newsboy's hand, staring off at the horizon meanwhile. Presently he would look down, and if the boy was gone he would ease on down the street with a contented smile. But if the boy was still there, actually hadn't made off with the change, he would frown; it was clear that he thought here was a boy with no red blood in his veins. The newsboys soon learned his desire with respect to the change, and saw that he was not disappointed.

Like all other cities of the time, Kansas City had its brothels. At Fourth and Wyandotte was the house of Annie Chambers, who catered to a free-spending clientele and offered "only the highest type girls." Annie Chambers was said to be descended from French nobility, which gave her house a touch of elegance, and she served fine wines in her expensively furnished rooms. She also had a reputation for philanthropy, as it was said that she employed "only professionals," and had helped many girls out of trouble. She once asked G. Van Millet, the city's leading artist, to paint portraits of her girls, and though he declined he later good-humoredly professed to regret his decision: "So many of our best citizens went down there . . . It would have been an excellent place to display my work . . . I would have had portrait commissions for the rest of my life."

One of the madams of the time even heckled the police commissioner in print. She had furnishings valued at eighteen thousand dollars in her house, and regarded it as superior to others. "If the police would let us sell beer and run our own dance halls we could pay big fines," she said. "Our big houses would be respectable and we could drive the cheap houses out of existence. What we need is a new police commissioner." Around 1900 there were one hundred and forty-seven houses, paying fines averaging $3,250 a month, each fine being in fact a recognized form of license fee. In the houses were 554 inmates, whose earnings averaged $49.35 a week, which they divided equally with the madams. A city ordinance, recognizing the actual situation and intended for enforcement, was worded briefly: "No woman under seventeen shall be tolerated in a bawdy house." Many well-meaning persons defended the operation of the houses, as being necessary to preserve respect for and virtue in decent womanhood. They contended, on what statistical grounds is unknown, that in towns which did not maintain brothels at least half the young girls were shameless.

There was not a public welfare department in the whole of the United States. Kansas City organized the first such department in 1908. The saloon crowd was dominant politically not only in the cattle-trading centers of the West, but also in the cities of the East. It was the day of the Thomas Nast cartoon. In Kansas City, there were six hundred saloons, or approximately three to every one thousand inhabitants. The downtown area was still a man's world, and brawling was frequent.

Under these circumstances, James Pendergast and his two brothers—Mike, who played a minor role as boss of the tenth ward, and Tom, who succeeded him in power—gained some part of their prestige from their physical prowess. They were not tall men, but they were broad-beamed and athletic. Brother Tom had attended St. Mary's College in Kansas, where he had played football and baseball, the latter well enough to receive an offer of $60 a month from the Texas League. He was similar in build and appearance to Babe Ruth, with tremendous shoulders and small, almost delicate hands. But those small hands could transport a terrific wallop.

Brother Tom's fistic ability became a legend chiefly because of one fight. The fight grew out of the fact that James Pendergast kept good saloons, and ordinarily did not serve more than two or three drinks to a customer. One day Fireman Jim Flynn, the prize fighter, entered one of the Pendergast saloons. He was welcome for a time, but presently was told that he had had his quota. The prize fighter became belligerent, and although Pendergast reminded him that there were six hundred other saloons, he refused to leave. "There's nobody big enough to put me out," he said. Brother Tom was then called upon to do the job. After fifteen minutes of battling, during which the thud of fist upon flesh resounded through the room and a few chairs and tables were smashed, Fireman Jim limped from the place, having had considerably the worst of it. Brother Tom reached for his apron and resumed his bartending.

This fight later on assumed unusual significance. Fireman Jim Flynn was the only man who had ever knocked out Jack Dempsey. The fight had taken place early in Dempsey's career, and had attracted no attention at the time, but when Dempsey became champion it was frequently recounted. Also recounted was the fact that Tom Pendergast had had the best of Fireman Jim Flynn. The barroom fight had not been staged according to Marquis of Queensberry rules, nor was Fireman Jim in condition to make his best showing; nevertheless what happened seemed to make Tom Pendergast the equal of Jack Dempsey, and there were many who thought he might have gone far in prize fighting or professional baseball if he had chosen either of those lines.

Neither of these sports was a first attraction for Brother Tom, whose interests were directed elsewhere. At this time Ed Corrigan of Kansas City was the "Race Horse King of America," and operated the City Park, Hawthorne, Engleside, Tanforan and Elm Ridge tracks. James Pendergast had the liquor concession at Elm Ridge track, and Brother Tom was the cashier at the concession. There he acquired the fever for horse-race betting which possessed him for the rest of his life.

For many years, however, Tom Pendergast's betting was merely a matter of placing two dollars on a horse now and then, and was of no importance to anyone in Kansas City. From the time he assumed the post as street commissioner in Mayor Reed's administration, it was recognized that he would succeed his brother in power. "He is no mere battler; he is a man of marked executive ability," said the *Star*. As early as 1902, the Kansas City *World* carried these prophetic lines: "One of the best known names in Kansas City is Pendergast. This is largely due, of course, to the puissance of Alderman James Pendergast in local circles political for the last ten or fifteen years. But the famous alderman's younger brother, Thomas, who has just stepped out of the office of superintendent of streets and into that of marshal of Jackson County, has been gathering quite a bunch of laurels of his own in the last few years. He is just turned thirty and there is every prospect that he is going to make a marked impression on the local history of the next decade or so."

During the Pendergast rise in Kansas City, the political picture in Missouri was changing. After its revival in 1872, the Democratic party continued to carry Missouri for thirty-two unbroken years, a long enough period to make its tenure seem permanent. However, Missouri was a border state, and the situation was never the same as in the Solid South. From early years, attempts had been made to make the ticket attractive to both Confederates and Union men. For instance, Governor Crittenden, a Union man, who offered the reward for the James boys, was given the governorship at a time when both Missouri senators, Cockrell and Vest, were Confederate veterans.

Individual public men sought to make themselves acceptable to both sides of the surviving war issue. Governor Crittenden, to balance the fact that he had been a Union man, would be sure to denounce "the infamous Drake constitution," the short-lived document which deprived the former Confederates of the vote during the first two elections after the war. General Jo Shelby, the Confederate cavalry hero, who served as United States marshal at Kansas City and was one of the four or five most influential political figures in the state, was careful to conciliate the Union side. Speaking to a new citizen who had come from Kansas, General Shelby would say: "Now John Brown, there was a man; he had the right idea. I was over there in Kansas, mixing in their elections, along with all the rest of 'em. But I didn't have any business there. John Brown taught us all a good lesson."

In addition to the effects of Missouri's divided allegiance in the war, the fact that the bulk of immigration was continually from the north and east had influence. More and more independent and Republican voters moved into the state. In the nineties, Missouri began to be listed as doubtful political territory. Theodore Roosevelt, in 1904, was the first Republican actually to carry Missouri. Thereafter Missouri was a pivotal state, Democratic in Democratic years and Republican in Republican years, with a record of voting for every winning presidential candidate. St. Louis, as in the earlier years, was a Republican city; while Kansas City on the whole remained a Democratic town—thanks, in part, to the yeoman work of the Pendergasts in getting out the vote and keeping it in line.

A great many tributes were paid to James Pendergast in his day, and they came from opponents as well as friends. His principal rival, Boss Shannon, would concede: "Jim Pendergast is a capable man; yes indeed, a very capable man." A Republican county chairman said: "Personally, Jim Pendergast is a man worth knowing, and having him for a friend is an asset greater than a pot of gold." "That he will be re-elected is a cinch; everyone in his ward knows it and is glad of it," the Democratic Kansas City *Times* was saying at one stage. The Republican *Journal* called him "an actual and active force in the community, and a big-hearted humanitarian." The independent *Star* said: "He is a man of immense force of character, transcendent ability as an organizer, and when he says a thing is so, it is."

Thomas T. Crittenden, Jr., a two-term mayor of Kansas City, suggested in his recollections that Kansas City's magnificent Union Station, built uptown after a tremendous grading project and after $50,000,000 had been spent improving Stilwell's "terminal railroad system," might be considered James Pendergast's memorial. This station, called the second largest in the world, was not completed until 1914, after Pendergast's death. But Crittenden pointed out that when James Pendergast still controlled the city council, he had favored the new plan, even though it meant the destruction of the old Union Depot in the West Bottoms and the ruin of Pendergast's remaining business interests there. The first actual Pendergast memorial, however, is a good deal less pretentious than the Union Station. It is a seated statue in Mulkey Square, where he sits in bronze looking out over the West Bottoms, now so thoroughly industrialized that most of the old precincts contain no voters.

James Pendergast had scarcely more than made his power secure than he began to speak of retirement. "This is my last turn in politics; I'm positively going to retire," he said in 1900. Later he was saying: "If I run again it won't be under packin' house rules; I'm too old"; and still later: "Take Brother Tom; he'll make a fine alderman, and he'll be good to the boys, just as I've been. Eighteen years of thankless work for the city, eighteen years of abuse; eighteen years of getting jobs for the push, is all the honor I want." He was not old in years, but was suffering from Bright's disease, an illness which enabled him to appear as a tower of physical strength when in fact he was a dying man. He finally did retire in 1910, and died in the following year, at the age of fifty-five.

The voters "took Brother Tom," who in 1910 was elected to the city council. Boss Shannon, wily as always, with his small but adroit Rabbit faction behind him, managed to keep "Brother Tom" in second place politically for a number of years. But Tom Pendergast was persistent, and he closely followed the precepts laid down by his brother. On his office wall hung a cartoon showing James Pendergast holding the votes of the first ward in a bag. Free Christmas dinners and Christmas baskets continued to be a memorial to James, and many of his activities were put on a mass production basis.

There was really only one major rule in Pendergast politics: Keep doing favors, for anyone and everyone, day in and day out, and harvest votes in return. Tom Pendergast persisted along this line after all the other old-time saloon bosses had disappeared from the American scene. Finally, when the political scenery was greatly changed and he stood as a rather strange survival from the past, circumstances favored him and he rose to the top. Before his dismal downfall, he was for a good many years the most powerful man in Missouri.

CHAPTER TWELVE

Temple of Justice

A BALLAD, POPULAR ALONG THE Missouri border, often recalled that "Jesse James had a wife to mourn for his life," and that he had "two children that were brave." These two children, a boy and a girl, grew to maturity in Kansas City.

The older Jesse James's bandit career had a remarkable way of cropping up to affect his son's life. When young Jesse reached the age of fifteen, he applied for work in a Kansas City law office. He gave his name as Jesse James, Jr. His prospective employer gave him an incredulous look, and said he was Thomas T. Crittenden, Jr., a son of the Missouri governor who offered the rewards which resulted in the elder Jesse's death. The junior Crittenden wrote to Mrs. James and asked her if she had any objection to her son's working for Crittenden. Mrs. James, being a mild person, had no objection, though the fiery grandmother, Mrs. Samuels, had some difficulty in accepting the situation.

After a year or two as office boy for the Crittendens, Jesse,

Jr., was employed as a stock-taker at the Armour Packing Company. He made a creditable record there. He and his mother and sister, Mary, lived in a small frame house, which he gradually paid for out of his wages.

Former Governor Crittenden and his sons, staunch Democrats, were anxious to be of further service to the Jameses and to show beyond doubt that there had been no ill will involved in offering the ill-fated rewards for the boy's father. In 1896, when Jesse, Jr., was 21 years old, the Crittendens arranged for him to receive the cigar and confection concession at the Kansas City courthouse. Independence always remained the official seat of Jackson County, but Kansas City built a "branch" courthouse, about twenty times larger than the official one at Independence. In this "branch," Jesse James, Jr., set up a cigar stand, and his earnings there were expected to make things easier for the bandit's widow and family.

But at the courthouse the younger James fell into association with a dubious police character known as "Quail Hunter" Jack Kennedy. This association led, in 1898, to his being suspected along with Kennedy and several others in connection with a train robbery which occurred just outside Kansas City. He was taken into custody while tending his cigar stand, and was placed in jail.

Mrs. Samuels, past seventy years old, was still active. The day of her grandson's arrest, she started from her home town of Kearney to visit Mrs. James and the grandchildren in Kansas City. Arriving a little before train time, she sat down to wait in the small Kearney railroad station. Her son Jesse had been dead sixteen years, and in the one hand that was left after the Pinkerton bomb explosion she held a bouquet of flowers picked from his grave. At that time his grave was still in the yard of the Samuels home, and as long as the season lasted it was always in some kind of bloom. This was October and the leaves were turning, but it was warm and the door to the railroad station was open. Mrs. Samuels suddenly sat up very straight when a newsboy looked in the door and called: "Read all about the train robbery—Jesse James arrested."

It seemed to the grandmother that the train would never reach Kansas City so she could learn the meaning of the news story. On arrival, she was met by Mrs. James and was soon told the details. The train robbery of which her grandson was accused had occurred at a junction called Leeds, eight miles south of Kansas City. The express car of a train on the siding had been blown open with dynamite, and a small amount of loot taken. It was scarcely the dramatic, rough-riding type of train robbery carried out by the older Jesse. In fact, in this case the robbers had made use of a buggy, but there was also some suggestion that young Jesse had made his escape on the bicycle which he used in going to and from the courthouse. Nevertheless, the charge was a serious one.

Young Jesse had been arrested on suspicion, but without a warrant being sworn out, and before being jailed had been taken to an apartment in the Westport section for questioning, all of which Mrs. Samuels regarded as highly suspicious and irregular—typical of detectives, whom she detested. She was in possession of all the facts, and was seething with indignation, when a reporter from the *Star* arrived to interview her.

"What do I think of the arrest of Jesse? What do I think of it?"—and she caught a few angry breaths. "It's an outrage, it's a shame! To think that a poor boy has been locked up for something he never did. He's as innocent as a babe. Why, if Jesse's guilty, then I'm guilty. I sat with him on the porch of his home the night of the robbery and heard the explosion. I said to Jesse, 'What's that cannon firing for?' Jesse replied that very likely there was some big news, or something of the sort."

She demanded to know why her grandson had been taken to an apartment in Westport before being taken to jail. The reporter replied that the detectives had wanted to question him, or in police terms to "sweat" him. "Humph! What queer business. Try to make a man tell something he doesn't know, do they? Well, they better try me. Six horse blankets wouldn't sweat anything out of me."

She considered a few moments, and then burst forth again in strong tones. "It's the detectives that has done all this. They're the ones, the rascals. What they won't do! See this?" —and she held up the stump of her right arm. "That's what the detectives did. They threw a bomb into my house; they shot off my arm and killed my poor little Archie, a little child. And do you suppose they would hesitate to arrest an innocent boy? No, no, they'd do anything; and a better boy never lived. Why, only the other day I said to Mr. Crittenden: 'Mr. Crittenden, you have known Jesse a long time and you know what he has been doing; you know what a good boy he has been and I wish you would keep him under your care. He's down there among strangers and he's still young.' And Mr. Crittenden said to me: 'Yes, Mrs. Samuels, I have known Jesse since he was my office boy, and I have yet to see the first step he has taken in the wrong.'"

Mrs. Samuels referred to the statement that Jesse might have used his bicycle, and said: "Oh, Lord, to think of it, a wheel! I thought those robbers used a buggy." She then reverted to the subject of detectives, and said there had been one snooping around the house the night of the robbery. "I think it was just before midnight that someone knocked at the door," she said. "I called out 'Mary, Jesse, someone's at the

door.' Mary answered me. She woke Jesse and he went to the
door in his night clothes and said 'Who's there?' The man
said he was looking for a party named Saunders, and Jesse
said he didn't know any such person. Now, the man who woke
us up was a detective, I'm sure. He was just trying to see if
Jesse was home. I wish I'd known then that he was a detective.
I'd have taken a broomstick and given it to him this way . . ."
(Here she showed how she would have clubbed the detective
both right and left.) "Then I'd have told him to git. I'd just
like to meet one of them detectives once."

But Jesse's grandmother presently subsided and was inclined to agree that the young man had fallen into bad
company. It didn't mean that he was guilty of anything, but
he shouldn't have been running around with "Quail Hunter"
Kennedy . "I'm sorry to hear that Jesse's been mixed up with
Kennedy's name; it's bad business," she said, and shook her
head over this. She was then taken somewhat aback when the
reporter questioned her about a strange bit of information.
Although never convicted, "Quail Hunter" Kennedy had been
arrested and held in jail three different times on charges of
train robbery. It seemed that among his visitors at the jail
had been none other than the elderly mother of the James
boys, Mrs. Samuels herself. Was it true that she had visited
him in jail and had talked to him "for an hour or two"?

"An hour or two? Law no. The smell of the place made me
sick and I left. I wasn't there more than ten or fifteen minutes.
I couldn't stand it any longer. Now, I want you to *distinctly*
understand that I'm no friend of Mr. Kennedy's. I just went
there to see him, and I saw him, and that's all. Why did I go?
Well, I thought his case sounded some like that of my own
boys. He was *accused* of a great deal, but nothing was *proved*
against him. Besides, as I told the man at the jail, I'd just like
to see once what a *real* train robber looks like."

"Quail Hunter" Jack Kennedy was so called because on one occasion when he was captured, on horseback, at three o'clock in the morning, with a pistol, a shotgun, a black mask, a set of false whiskers and other paraphernalia in his possession, he claimed he was "going quail hunting." He had grown up a few miles southeast of Independence, in the "Cracker Neck" district, settled originally by poor whites from North Carolina. The region was hilly and wooded, with winding roads and tangled jungles of underbrush, and in the border and bandit days had been a favorite hiding place and rendezvous for the James and Younger boys. It included Blue Cut, a railroad pass where the James boys staged one of their first and one of their last train robberies. The weather-stained frame house of the Kennedys stood on a knoll overlooking Blue Cut, where the "Quail Hunter" had played along the track as a boy. Like every other boy of the time, he heard many stories about the James and Younger boys, and he developed a great admiration for them.

For some reason, he never outgrew it. Although his father placed him in a good job on a railroad, and he actually worked himself up to the position of engineer, he sometimes let it be known that he regarded railroading as merely preliminary training for a career as a train robber. It was known, too, that he had long paid court to Maggie Ralston; and that his attraction to her, originally at least, was based on the fact that she was a relative of Frank James. "Jesse James, Frank James and the Younger bandits are his patron saints; he worships them," said the *Star*, in an article seeking to explain his career.

In 1896, he quit his job on the railroad, collected a band, and staged two train holdups in Blue Cut. He did not get much the first time, but obtained $32,000 the second. He was arrested both times, and acquitted. His story around town was that it cost him the entire $32,000 to win the second case. He once borrowed $50 from a bartender with the statement that the "boys" were going to "turn over" a train the following night. He seemed very anxious to build his reputation as a bandit.

To get the son of Jesse James into his band became his ambition. So when young Jesse opened his cigar stand, Kennedy began hanging around it, and struck up an acquaintance. He was so successful in winning the friendship he sought that young Jesse, even after he was in deep trouble, was saying: "Kennedy is a friend of mine, and I don't give a damn who knows it."

After the train robbery at Leeds, a member of the band was picked up. He had in his pocket a note signed "Jesse James," which arranged for a meeting. This bandit made an alleged confession in which he named young Jesse as one of the five or six robbers. At this point Jesse was arrested, without the formality of a warrant.

Members of the Southern element were highly critical of the manner in which he was taken into custody. Former Governor Crittenden vigorously denounced it, declaring: "The arrest of Jesse James is a greater crime than train robbery. If I were governor, I would have the men who arrested him indicted." Judge John W. Henry summed up the sentiments of many when he said: "The manner in which this boy has been kidnapped by the police is a damnable outrage."

"You must bear in mind," Judge Henry continued, "that young Jesse James is not like other boys. He occupies a peculiar position in this community. His father was a bandit and was killed for a reward. Young Jesse has grown up here, watched by everybody. Many have watched over him with a solicitude for his welfare, advising him, guiding his footsteps in the right, anxious for him to get along and be a good man. I

Jesse James at the time of the Civil War

have watched this boy closely and I know that no boy in the country has led a better life. He has worked and saved and alone and unaided has paid for the home in which he, his mother and his sister live. It was his money that clothed his sister and paid for her music lessons. No one ever saw this boy in a saloon. Here he has grown up with us, with all his father's past to live down, and I say he has shown himself to be a well-balanced, worthy boy. To brand that boy as a train robber would be a crime that would merit hanging."

"The arrest of young Jesse James," said the *Star*, "has aroused and stirred up that element of the community which is linked by old memories with the border days, when the people of this county were divided on the issues of the Civil War. Older men with excited faces and eyes flashing with anger appeared at police headquarters and around the jail early this morning, and demanded to know where was Jesse James and by what authority he was held. The voices of these men trembled with excitement as they talked about the case. At the courthouse police were denounced for making the arrest. Many of the people employed there made light of the claim that they had a strong case, and it was evident that, guilty or guiltless, Jesse James had friends there. The arrest was spoken of by some as a very serious mistake, for it would be 'bad for the party.' "

A man named David Ball, described in the papers as "a candidate for the Democratic nomination for governor," came all the way from Pike County to offer to act free of charge as Jesse's attorney. His services were refused, as the defendant already had three attorneys active in his behalf. One of them said: "I think the police made a mistake in the way they went about arresting James. It has, however, done him no harm, for it has aroused the feelings of many good persons who will interest themselves in his case. Why, do you know that Jesse James can give bond right now for a million dollars? It's a fact. The public would be surprised to know the names of wealthy men who have come to me and offered to sign his bond. They know the boy's good reputation and believe he is innocent. Why, Mr. Swinney (a Kansas City banker) voluntarily offered to sign his bond because he lives near Jesse and knows what kind of a boy he is."

The first hearing was before Judge Henry himself, on a writ of habeas corpus. Judge Henry's first remark to the attorney from the prosecutor's office was: "What have you to say for yourself, Mr. Lowe?" The judge was clearly in no mood for trifling in this case. Mr. Lowe read a statement from the police commissioner to the effect that Jesse James was held on the strength of another's confession implicating him in the train robbery. The defense then moved the prisoner's release. "It has never been the custom—" began Mr. Lowe, at which the defense interrrupted with, "It's law we're after here, not custom."

"Let Mr. Lowe proceed," said Judge Henry. "Go on, Mr. Lowe."

"I wanted to say that it has been the custom here for many years for the police, when a party is suspected of a crime, to take him into custody for investigation. This is the first case I have known in fifteen years where an attempt has been made to disturb that custom." To this the defense replied: "Be it custom or not, the young man is held without right or process of law. If the police have evidence, let them swear out a warrant like men."

Mr. Lowe made what the *Star* described as "an ineffectual attempt to say something more about the custom," but Judge Henry had had enough, and silenced him. "I am surprised, Mr. Lowe, that you would appear in this court to defend a custom that is not backed up by law. For six hundred years the English-speaking people have enjoyed freedom of person. The police have no right to arrest any man without a warrant because they merely suspect him of a crime. The practice which seems to be in vogue here of arresting a man on suspicion and holding him until they can extort from him a confession or procure testimony against him is not to be tolerated. It is well enough that we understand this thing now and for all. And there is a higher law even than the law of the state or even the United States, and that is the Constitution of the United States." Judge Henry read pertinent sections of the Constitution, regarding due process of law and freedom from search and seizure. He then slammed the book shut, took off his spectacles and pronounced: "The prisoner is released."

While the hearing was in progress, the police had taken the trouble to swear out a warrant, and it was served on Jesse before he could walk out of the courtroom. However, he was merely taken down the hall to another court, and released on $2,500 bond. As he approached his cigar stand, an elevator boy held up a copy of the *Star*, which contained seven columns of the case, including three columns on the front page, and said: "Gee, I'll bet you sell a thousand dollars' worth of cigars today. You sold twenty dollars' worth after you left the first day." "Kennedy has instilled some bad ideas into the boy's head and made him think that by right of his father's notoriety he is something of a hero," said the *Star*. "But Jesse is very popular at the courthouse, and previous to this has cared nothing for personal notice."

About one hundred witnesses were summoned by each side for the trial of Jesse, Jr. The courtroom was filled to the doors every day. "There have been other remarkable trials," said the *Star*, "but in all these other trials the courtroom was filled with a hodgepodge audience of all sorts of persons, who seemed to have come from mere curiosity and were ready to

laugh at the most trivial thing. But in this trial of Jesse James
every one of the hundreds in the courtroom seems to have a
personal interest in it. They watch things so closely. The
feelings of suspense seem to fill the very air of the crowded
room. The looks of deep attentive concern on every face are
quite wonderful to see. There is no levity, no laughter, and
there are no interruptions."

There was probably not a man in the courtroom, or any
deep-dyed son of the Missouri border, who did not know
passages by heart from the famous editorial written by Major
John N. Edwards on the death of the senior Jesse James—the
editorial which ended with: ". . . a brazen harlot, naked to
the waist and spattered to the brows with blood!" So Attorney
Walsh had no need to say whom he was paraphrasing when
he concluded the defense of young Jesse by exclaiming:
"What a spectacle! Missouri, with all her order, progress and
development. Missouri, with every screw and cog and crank
and lever and wheel of her administrative machinery in
perfect working order. Is it possible that this great commonwealth had to ally itself with hired detectives, with paid
bloodhounds of the law, that the majesty of the law might be
vindicated? This trial means more than the mere fate of this
boy. If you convict him we might as well tear the two bears
from the flag of Missouri, and put thereon, in place of them, as
more appropriate, the leering face of a detective and the
crawling, snake-like shape of an informer!"

The jury went out to dinner and on its return found the
defendant not guilty. The verdict was received with a burst
of handclapping, stamping and whistling. One of the pleased
faces in the courtroom was that of former Governor Crittenden, who had taken a strong stand against the activities of
Jesse James, but who now wholeheartedly defended his son.
By this time there were eight indictments in the train robbery,

but Prosecutor Reed moved to dismiss them all. "We have just presented what we considered our strongest case, as far as evidence was concerned," he said, "and we have concluded that it would be a useless expense to try the others."

Young Jesse James was never again in trouble. He saved his money, in the course of time was admitted to the bar, and eventually left Missouri and settled in California.

It would be an exaggeration of the importance of young Jesse James's trial to say that it served as a springboard for two remarkable careers. Nevertheless, the facts remain that both of the leading attorneys in the case did achieve national prominence, and that the rivalry between these two attorneys became almost as legendary as the story of the original Jesse James. The attorneys were James A. Reed, the prosecutor, subsequently mayor of Kansas City and a United States senator; and Frank P. Walsh, chief of the battery of defense counsel, who later served twenty years as attorney for Tom Mooney.

Reed, a fiery conservative, spent eighteen years in the Senate, was one of the two or three men most instrumental in defeating American entry into the League of Nations, and afterward twice had Missouri's endorsement for the Democratic presidential nomination. Walsh, a liberal, achieved a national reputation as chairman of the Commission on Industrial Relations, which was created by Congress in 1913 to inquire into the causes of industrial unrest. He subpoenaed J. P. Morgan, John D. Rockefeller, and Andrew Carnegie, among others, for hearings that drew headlines in 1913 and 1914; and he afterward was co-chairman of the War Labor Board in the first World War. Walsh's unusual personal qualities were shown by the fact that he became a close friend both of the conservative William Howard Taft, who served with him on the War Labor Board, and of Franklin D. Roosevelt, founder of the New Deal.

These aspects in the careers of Walsh and Reed largely concerned the nation. But before they emerged on the national scene they conducted a long legal and political feud in Kansas City, beginning with the Jesse James trial. Reed was attorney for the Metropolitan Street Railway Company, and Walsh brought a record number of damage actions against him. Their rivalry had the effect of increasing the practices of both, since it became a matter of established precedent that when one of the two men was engaged on a case, the other automatically was retained to oppose him. "I'm raising eight children by practicing law against Jim Reed," Walsh used to say. Reed and Walsh were "the best lawyers in town."

Although both were Democrats, their rivalry was political as well as legal because of the two factions. Reed was the principal candidate and speaker of the Pendergast Goats, whereas Walsh was the advisor and strategist of the Shannon Rabbits.

The legal phase of the Walsh-Reed feud culminated in 1910, when they were opposing attorneys in the Swope murder trial. This was one of the most spectacular murder cases in the country's history, and it had the full attention of all newspapers of the time. In addition to providing a baffling mystery which was never entirely solved, it was in a sense a genuinely historic case for Kansas City. For the corpus delicti concerned the body of Colonel Thomas H. Swope, who when the land was barren had owned the acres on which the Kansas City business district took form, and who, as the possessor of millions, had figured so largely in the city's development.

CHAPTER THIRTEEN

Too Far Out

COLONEL SWOPE WAS A GENTLE, sorrowful man, who saw extraordinary events, and who was continually doctoring himself for dyspepsia. Back when the steamboat cargoes were arriving at a rate of six or seven hundred a year and the wagon freight was piled all along the river front from Main to Delaware streets, Colonel Swope was selling lots and complaining of his dyspepsia. When the front of the town shifted to the West Bottoms and the business district grew up on his property, he appeared more interested in his dyspepsia than in his good fortune. When Kansas City came of age in 1900 (the year that the city built a big auditorium in ninety days and was host to the second of the Democratic conventions that nominated Bryan), Colonel Swope was still on hand and taking medicines for dyspepsia. Even in his death that ailment figured, because in doctoring for dyspepsia he took a tonic which contained a small quantity of strychnine.

Swope was elderly at the time of his death, and his life went back almost to the beginning of the city. He had received a small inheritance from his Kentucky forebears, had attended Yale University, and had come west again in 1855. That was when the Kansas Territory was being opened, and Kansas City was on the verge of a rapid growth; but at the moment of his arrival it listed a population of only four hundred and forty-two people, who were living in houses perched on clifftops or huddled under bluffs. Colonel Swope saw that, since the river lay to the north, the town must grow toward the south. So he bought a rugged farm for $7,500, immediately south of the levee district, and divided it into lots. The city did grow to the south, the farm became its million-dollar acres of steel and concrete, and Colonel Swope became a multimillionaire.

These developments made it appear that Colonel Swope had shown great foresight. But Colonel Swope himself always denied that he had shown any foresight, and in fact regarded his entire fortune as accidental. When he had cut the farm into lots, he had had the idea that he was creating a residential district, which might not even be a very prosperous one. When opportunities came, he sold his lots for small profits of one, two or three hundred dollars. Then he lived to see some of the lots valued at a quarter to a half million dollars. Most of the property he owned later, he had had to repurchase at prices much higher than those at which he had sold.

Looking back over his life, it seemed to Colonel Swope that he should have known the business district would locate on his land, and that he should have known which of the lots would become valuable. He was perfectly honest and straight-thinking to the end, but a bit eccentric in his later years; and he was given to waggling his head as he walked along the streets, and to muttering and repeating within the hearing of those about him: "You're an old fool, Tom Swope; yes sir, an old fool." Sometimes he would look up at the tall buildings around him and repeat in clear tones: "Yes sir, an old fool." One day a friend stopped to remonstrate that he could scarcely be an old fool, since he had become the town's richest man. "I think you've been pretty smart," said the friend. Colonel Swope was not in the least taken aback. He seemed to accept it as perfectly natural that an outside voice should intrude upon his thoughts. But he placed both hands on top of his cane and eyed the friend coldly. "Me, smart?" he queried, as though a more preposterous proposition had never been posed. Then with one arm he swept the downtown area. "I owned all of downtown, almost, and I sold it off for a few hundred dollars an acre. I have never done a day's work in my life; I have never earned a dollar in my life. You say I am rich, and that is true, but do you know why?" Here Colonel Swope looked up again at the buildings around him, and waggled his head sadly. "There were two of these lots I couldn't sell. One was a hole in the ground, and the other was an ugly clay hill. Nobody would give me anything for them, nobody thought they were worth anything, so I kept them—and they made me rich. That is no credit to me." The two lots to which he referred had become the sites of office buildings, and each was paying him a ground rental of $50,000 a year, or thereabouts. He considered them the whole basis of his fortune.

In his later years the thought that he had made his wealth so easily and accidentally, while others had worked hard for meager returns, sometimes weighed on Colonel Swope's mind. Through most of his life he had been close-fisted. Frequently at a bar he would order two drinks of whisky and say he would be back later for the second, in order to take advantage of the two-for-a-quarter price, and he was habitually very austere when appeals for charity were made. Then he took to presenting a ten-dollar bill each morning to his cousin and business manager, Colonel Moss Hunton, with instructions to use the money to help someone in need. Since both lived in a good residential district, Colonel Hunton experienced some difficulty in getting rid of the ten dollars a day. He finally adopted the practice of filling his pockets each morning with candy and chewing gum, and buying an armful of flowers; and then passing these out along the streets as the first exercise in his day's work. This daily ritual made Colonel Hunton a familiar figure in the neighborhood for a number of years.

Colonel Swope more than suspected that his ten dollars a day was not reaching the really poor, who he discovered existed in large numbers in other parts of the city, and he long considered some larger and more expansive public benefaction. But he could not quite bring himself to part with a substantial portion of his fortune, and always found some reason for not doing so. For a long time he thought he would build a large public library. One day he went down and stood outside the public library, and it seemed to him that everyone entering and leaving was fairly well dressed, so he abandoned the project. Then he was caught by the force of Nelson's campaign for public parks. Nelson was blasting at what he once called "the pinching economy, the picayunish policy, the miserable parsimony which characterize our city government." The Park Board was anxious to make an expansive showing. Colonel Swope owned or could buy the plots included in two square miles of pasture land southeast of town. The Park Board considered this land ideal for a public park which would complete its system of parks. Colonel Swope was put under great pressure to donate the tract. This he did, in 1896, when he was approaching his seventieth year.

The ground for Swope Park, which stands today as the third largest municipal park in America, was cut by the Blue River, an exceptionally winding stream, bordered by broad flood plains, from which rose steep and thickly wooded uplands. The variation in terrain was ideal for a park, and his gift was accepted with the greatest enthusiasm. Although Swope's land was assessed at only one hundred dollars an acre, it was estimated that the park might some day be the equal of New York's Central Park, which for local purposes was valued at four hundred million dollars. A procession and Jubilee Day was arranged for the dedication of the park. Nelson, in his usual directorial vein, stated flatly in his newspaper that every man, woman, and child should immediately begin making arrangements to be present for the Jubilee. Eighteen thousand people followed his instructions, and more would have done so if there had been sufficient means of transportation to the place.

Colonel Swope was scheduled to ride in a carriage with the mayor at the head of the procession. At the last moment, he was overcome by modesty. Instead of riding in the carriage, he struck out on foot, cutting across fields to reach the park, which was about seven miles from the center of the business district. Thus the donor of the park arrived on foot for its dedication, while the recipients were coming in a procession of carriages, wagons, horsemen, and bicyclists that stretched all the way back to town. On another side of the park, overloaded steam trains were arriving, with passengers riding on the tops of cars and even on coal tenders.

Since the greater part of Kansas City's population was fairly new to the place, and since Colonel Swope was a retiring man, he was largely unnoticed in the crowd. "Thousands were wondering where was Mr. Swope," said the *Star*. He was there, wandering about, musing in his usual way.

He watched the crowd around the small railroad station, which looked like a floating island bobbing up and down in a sea of people. He listened to the medley of music which came from a dancing platform and from three bandstands, with military bands. Then from one speaking platform he heard Judge John W. Henry, the same Judge Henry who was so stirred by the Jesse James case, reading a whereas, whereas and whereas resolution to the effect that a statue of Colonel Swope should be erected. From another platform he heard Mayor Jones saying: "Mr. Swope is a great public benefactor; his name will live and the Swope Jubilee will serve as a milestone in the city's march of progress." Above a third platform Colonel Swope saw a seven-foot likeness of himself, made by a local artist, and inscribed WELCOME.

The crowds were patrolled by Marshal Hale's firemen in red and white sashes. The firemen had won honors at the Paris Exposition and were considered a great advertisement for the city. Everyone wore ribboned badges which read: ALL HONOR TO THOMAS H. SWOPE. In the valleys people gathered armloads of purple sumac blossoms and black-eyed susans. Said the *Star:* "It was grand, astonishing and numerous . . . The crowds were happy, panoramic and many-hued." Someone who did recognize him mentioned to Colonel Swope that several thousand people could not get there because of the overcrowded trains. "Too bad, too bad; I wish they could all come," said the colonel mournfully. Then he straightened up with what, for Colonel Swope, was quite an expansive gesture, and said: "It does me good to see all these people out here."

The skies darkened and a few drops of rain fell, but the clouds were providentially borne off to the horizon by a stiff breeze. When the crowd had fully gathered, there was a flag-raising ceremony. Battery B of the Missouri Guard

fired a forty-four gun salute in honor of Colonel Swope. There
were more speeches and more cheering. Because of his
obscurity in the crowd, Colonel Swope could not be located
for newspaper comment until some time after the ceremonies,
when he was found back at his office. But when he was
located, he wrote the following statement, which was re-
produced in large facsimile on the *Star's* front page: "I have
often heard it said that gratitude is a scarce article in this
world, but from this time on I shall reject and ignore that
pessimistic sentiment."

As time passed, however, there was some criticism of the
park. The city usually spent from fifty to seventy-five thousand dollars a year on its improvement and maintenance,
and there was some objection to this expense. More frequent
was the objection that the park was "too far out." It was then
thought of as being three or four miles out in the country,
and the only means of getting there was a branch of Stilwell's
"Air Line" railway, or by horse and buggy.

Once he had bestowed the gift, Swope Park was the pride
and monument of the colonel's life. Every word of criticism
wounded him to the soul. Consequently, in addition to
muttering "You're an old fool, Tom Swope," he was sometimes
heard to mutter "too far out, too far out, too far out," meanwhile swishing his cane in impatience at the thought.

To scotch the idea that Swope Park was "too far out"
became a mild obsession with the colonel. He grew more
optimistic about the city's future than he had ever been in
the real-estate business. He was a slender man, bald except
for a fringe, with wide-set eyes that gave him a somewhat
child-like appearance despite the mustache he wore. Leaning
with one arm on a bar, he would say: "Young man, has it

ever occurred to you that the cities of the Old World grew to a half million before the days of railroads? Kansas City is in the center of the richest agricultural section of the United States. I won't see it, but you will live to see more than a million people here; perhaps two million. Believe me, Swope Park is none too far out."

The same theme crept into a plan which he long entertained for building an art museum. "I have visited various cities in the East with an architect, and have given a great deal of time and study to the subject," he said. "After careful investigation I decided I would like to reproduce the Albright Gallery of Buffalo, but with Vermont marble as the material. The Albright Gallery was designed by a commission which visited Europe, and is supposed to represent a combination of the best the commission saw abroad. I have reserved five acres at the entrance to Swope Park as a site for the museum. Some people say it is too far out. Now,"—and here Colonel Swope picked up his drink with a gesture which indicated he was getting to the point—"I have carefully looked into the matter of damage to pictures and books and other things from the smoke and dust and bad atmosphere of cities, and the loss is *something enormous.* You can take my word for it, Swope Park is none too far out."

Through most of his life, Colonel Swope drank steadily. Some people, before visiting his office, watched his trips to the saloon, believing that the best time to see him was between the first and second drinks, or between the third and fourth. It was stated for the record at the later trial that he had been intoxicated every afternoon for twenty-five years, but that was an exaggeration. Moreover, he must have had iron in his will power, for eventually he did what few hard drinkers of his age have been able to do: at eighty-one he quit drinking altogether. Although he grew much weaker and several doctors told him it would be better if he drank moderately, he never took another drop.

But he could not avoid mental depressions. Once he was started in philanthropy, he bestowed a great many gifts on various institutions, but none of these gifts produced the high enthusiasm or the wonderful tribute of the Jubilee Day at Swope Park. Sometimes Colonel Swope planned to expand his charities, and sometimes he thought he would never make another donation as long as he lived. "I am rich," he said, "but I'm alone in the world. Nobody invites me to his home. Nobody wants to see me. Nobody comes to my office except to ask for something. I have given ground for institutions now known in the names of other men; I don't care about that, but who remembers those gifts?" In this mood, on Dec. 5, 1904, he addressed a brief letter to a Kansas City minister:

Dear Mr. Northrup:
I would have answered your letter, but really I do not know what to say—except to say that I cannot share your enthusiasm in good works. You no doubt love your fellow men; I do not, and this (my care) is one of the evil consequences of riches—wrong, injustice and robbery have hardened my heart.
Yours sincerely,
Thos. H. Swope

Colonel Swope was alone in the sense of having no one to share his old age, but he was a part of a very large household. Himself a lifelong bachelor, he had a brother who married and had seven children. When the family was about half grown, the brother died. The widow and seven children lived in Independence, in a large house with a tower and battlements. The house sat on the highest point of nineteen acres of ground and was surrounded by tall elms, gardens and winding walks—one of the most imposing of residences. Although it took him nearly an hour to travel from that part of Independence to downtown Kansas City via the streetcar, Colonel Swope moved to the home of the other Swope family at the time of his brother's death. Thereafter, he was a rich uncle living in a room upstairs.

In drawing his will, Colonel Swope thought first of these seven nephews and nieces. By specific bequests, he left them enough property to provide each with an income of $12,000 a year. There remained in his estate a residuary, valued at $1,400,000, for which no specific provision was made. It was Colonel Swope's intention to give this money away while he still lived, and thus to enjoy whatever festivities might accompany the giving. As the end of his life approached without his having given the money away, he also talked at times of leaving it in a charitable trust. But if he died suddenly without effecting his charitable intentions, the nephews and nieces were also the heirs to the residuary part of his estate. From the standpoint of the nephews and nieces, the arrangement placed a premium on his sudden death; but the Swopes were a devoted family, and this thought seems never to have occurred either to Colonel Swope or to any of the many persons with whom he discussed his will.

In 1905, about the time the colonel was drawing his last will, one of the Swope daughters fell in love with Dr. Bennett Clark Hyde, a man of whom her mother did not approve. Dr. Hyde was an intelligent young man, a graduate of William Jewell College, and son of a minister. But Mrs. Swope said she "had it very straight" that her daughter's suitor had been making love to other and older women, and then borrowing money from them, which he neglected to repay. She was able to name two women, and the amounts of money borrowed, $4,000 in one case and $2,200 in the other.

Young Dr. Hyde's lawyer came to see Mrs. Swope. He admitted his client's affairs with the other two women, but denied that there had been any such financial transactions as were reported to her. Mrs. Swope remained unreconciled, but the engagement was announced. When one of the "other women" threatened to sue Dr. Hyde, the engagement was broken off. Then in June, 1905, the daughter and Dr. Hyde eloped to Arkansas and were married. For nearly a year the two families were estranged. Then Dr. Hyde fell ill, Mrs. Hyde called in Mrs. Swope, and they were reconciled. Through all this Colonel Swope followed the lead of his sister-in-law, Mrs. Swope. He strongly disapproved of Dr. Hyde when she did, and became reconciled to him when Mrs. Swope accepted the situation.

After the reconciliation, Colonel Swope thought he should do something for the young couple. He decided to give them a $7,500 house. With furnishings and other expenses, the total cost came to $10,000, so he presented Dr. Hyde with a check for that amount. Dr. Hyde seemed quite appreciative. Colonel Swope was encouraged to say that if Dr. Hyde made good, he would do a good deal more for him. Dr. Hyde again was appreciative and said he would certainly do his best. They talked for an hour or two, and Colonel Swope came away feeling that he had done well with at least that much of his money.

The gift wrought a wonderful change in Colonel Swope. Previously he had been lukewarm, at best, toward his niece's husband. Now he would hear nothing against him. Colonel Swope had influence wherever a bequest might fall, and he obtained for Dr. Hyde an appointment to the staff at City Hospital. He thought of him as a smart man and a rising physician, and he liked him personally. Out of the attachment which the Colonel formed for his nephew-in-law came the fact that, although Dr. Hyde was not the Swope family physician, he was Colonel Swope's physician in the colonel's last illness.

At the time of the reconciliation in 1906, Colonel Swope was approaching eighty, and from that time on was much concerned about his will. Frequently he would take the will from his office safe, and bring it home week ends for study. Sometimes he would try to tinker with the special bequests, saying that real-estate values were changing, and that he wanted to be fair to everybody. Then he would declare that if he changed it a hundred times, he could not make it any better. Incidentally, despite his own opinion to the contrary, Colonel Swope was an excellent judge of real estate, in a way that was difficult to explain. He was intuitively shrewd, with an immediate grasp of the essential facts of a situation, though with little ability to base his judgment on a reasoning process.

As for the residuary part of his wealth, Colonel Swope could not work out an arrangement that satisfied him. If he left the residue to the city, he said, it would be "eaten up by a bunch of politicians." If he left it in charge of businessmen, they would "huckster it about from one real-estate office to another until there was nothing left." If he left it in charge of lawyers—Colonel Swope shuddered at the thought. Once he said he had decided what to do with the residuary, without saying which plan he meant. But it may reasonably be doubted whether Colonel Swope ever would have disposed of the matter, however long he lived, for the truth was that the business of trying to decide how to bestow his wealth provided his principal reason for existence in his last years.

That and reading. He read a great deal, and his reactions were unpredictable. After someone sent him a set of Balzac, Colonel Swope declared: "Balzac was a great literary genius, but these books are dangerous! They are immoral; they will have an evil influence. I am going to burn them." He thought better of burning them, but approached Dr. Jacob Billikopf, who was head of the Jewish Educational Institute and sometimes talked to him about the advantages of dedicating his wealth to public purposes. "Now, you're a man of good strong moral character," the colonel began—and Dr. Billikopf acquired a set of Balzac. In reading a romantic novel, Colonel Swope came upon a place where the hero was made to tell a lie, and he immediately threw the book aside. "A lie by the hero might be permissible in realistic literature, but in the romantic—never." He was on page 189 of a 200-page book when this happened, but said afterward that he hadn't finished the book and never would. He began reading the essays of a British writer, A. C. Benson, because he understood that Benson was an elderly bachelor like himself; and these essays at the last were his favorite reading matter.

After he quit drinking he became so weak that it was usually necessary for someone to help him on and off streetcars. Colonel Swope's office was in the New England Building; he took a streetcar which passed that place and transferred at Tenth and Grand to the Independence car. He had an office associate, Sylvester V. Spangler, who each afternoon put him on the streetcar. Spangler would start to get aboard to help him make his transfer, but Colonel Swope invariably would wave him back, saying: "That will be all, Spangler. You go on back to the office. I can make my transfer all right." Spangler, after eyeing his decrepit charge with much less confidence in his ability to make his transfer, would then hurry on foot over a short cut to the transfer point, and would be waiting when the colonel arrived. Colonel Swope would get off creakily, and climb aboard the Independence car with a parting injunction that it would be entirely unnecessary to meet him the next day; but the next morning Spangler would again be at the transfer point.

Colonel Swope continued to come to his office in this fashion for nearly a year. One day in early September, 1909, a friend told him he was looking well. Colonel Swope said, "Oh, yes," in an abrupt, nervous way, as though to dismiss the matter. Then he turned around, peered closely at the friend, and replied more fully, saying he certainly did not *feel* well. "We've had a warm summer; you'll feel better now that fall has come," said the friend. Colonel Swope would not be encouraged. "You remind me of what they told me when I felt bad last winter. 'When spring and summer come,' they said, 'you will feel better.' I'm getting too far along for that now. My nervous system is badly shattered and I suffer so intensely all the time that I expect to be dead and buried within ninety days."

The conversation continued, and presently, without rancor, almost as though he were speaking of someone else, Colonel Swope was saying: "If I do not die within ninety days, I shall be very much surprised—and a little disappointed. I am perfectly ready and willing to die. Life has held few pleasures for me, and fewer are left now. I'm tired of people and more tired of myself. I read a great deal just to keep my mind off myself. I must surely gain more by death than I will lose."

Thirty days later he was dead, and Kansas City was asking for a public funeral. The relatives agreed, and the body was turned over to a committee headed by Mayor Crittenden.

A last tribute was then paid to the man whose name, because of the big park, would always be closely associated with that of the city. He lay in state at the Public Library. At the head of the casket stood a ten-foot pillar formed of three thousand carnations, and twined around the pillar were wreaths of roses and lilies of the valley which spelled out,

KANSAS CITY MOURNS. All the church bells tolled. The schools were closed, and the children, monitored by their teachers, were lined up along the route of the funeral march, from the Public Library to Grace Episcopal Church. The police, the National Guard, the fire department, all city departments and all lodges, and labor and commercial organizations were represented in the procession. Colonel Swope's funeral procession, taking forty-five minutes to pass a given point, was the longest procession of any kind that the city had seen.

Conspicuous among the mourners was Dr. Bennett Clark Hyde, solemn as he followed the casket up the church aisle, with his veiled wife on his arm. It was not until three months later that there was any suspicion of the part Dr. Hyde had played in the colonel's death. Colonel Swope's body was placed temporarily in a cemetery vault, until a tomb could be prepared in Swope Park, where he had asked to be buried.

CHAPTER FOURTEEN

House of Death

PEOPLE FOUND IT DIFFICULT to explain the character-istics that struck them as odd in Dr. Hyde. All agreed that he was impressive. He was well-built and erect, and proud to the point of being haughty. He wore nose glasses; his hair was parted in the middle and inclined to fall forward; he had a broad face, a strong chin, a wide mouth and an engaging smile; and when his smile was at its best, his eyes grew positively moist.

And yet there were times when it seemed as though his mind had directed his face to smile. Then in some discon-certing moment, when there should be a spontaneous reaction, there was nothing; he was absolutely cold unless and until he decided to change his expression.

Not that he was slow-witted. On the contrary, he was ex-ceptionally sharp. It was simply that the responses which in most people occur more or less automatically, in him came only from the conscious side. He gave the impression that he never so much as flickered an eyelash unless there was some purpose in doing so.

For all that, Dr. Hyde had friends as well as enemies. He was well-mannered, well-read, abreast of his profession, and informed on politics and sports. After his reconciliation with the Swopes, things went smoothly for nearly three years. The Hydes were usually at the Swope home in Independence for Sunday dinner, and sometimes they were there during the week. If Mrs. Swope went out of town, the Hydes usually stayed at the Swope home so that Mrs. Hyde could take charge of the big house.

In addition to the widowed Mrs. Swope and the four daughters and one son who were living at home, the household included Colonel J. Moss Hunton, a man of much patience and indulgence, who was a sort of father confessor to the family, and Colonel Swope's business manager. The daughters were from fourteen to twenty-three years old, and frequently brought other girls home to spend the night. A seamstress stayed part of the time. There was a colored woman cook, and a colored housegirl. Relatives from out of town often visited. Then, before his death, there was Colonel Swope himself—Uncle Thomas out here—who came down for meals but usually kept to his room. The family said he was eccentric and didn't like company, which was his claim, although those who persisted found him glad enough to talk.

On September 6, 1909, two days after he had predicted his own death, Colonel Swope fell in his room and injured one shoulder. Dr. G. T. Twyman of Independence, the family physician, was called but was out on a case. His son, Dr. Elmer Twyman, came and found that Colonel Swope was not badly hurt. But the fall was a shock for a man eighty-two years old, and Colonel Swope remained in bed. In a few days, Dr. Hyde came out. Dr. Hyde had frequently gone out of his way to talk to the colonel, showing him much more attention than did the Swopes. On this occasion he spent an hour or two with him. Colonel Swope was glad to talk. He accepted Dr. Hyde's medical counsel, and told him of his latest plan for changing his will. Following the talk, Dr. Hyde assumed full responsibility as Colonel Swope's physician, and ordered a trained nurse to attend him. The nurse arrived on September 12.

The next day, on September 13, Dr. Hyde called Brecklein's Drug Store and ordered four five-grain capsules of cyanide of potassium to be sent to his office and charged to his account. It was a surprising order. The textbooks described five grains of cyanide as a lethal dose for an adult human being. The store had never before sold cyanide to a physician; and, although it had sold a good deal in bulk to jewelers, photographers and dentists, it had never before sold any in capsules. Nevertheless, one of the employees took a druggist's mortar, powdered some cyanide crystals, filled the capsules and had them delivered to Dr. Hyde. The following day Dr. Hyde bought a box of Holloden digestive capsules, which in appearance could not be distinguished from the cyanide.

Nothing unusual occurred for two weeks. Then on October 1, Colonel Moss Hunton had an apoplectic stroke while seated at the Swope dinner table. "Things look queer to me; what's the matter?" he said. With difficulty he raised a glass of water to his lips. The glass fell back in his plate, and the family rushed to his aid. He was placed on a cot. One side was paralyzed, and he was unconscious. Dr. Twyman was called and arrived first; the Hydes were called and arrived soon afterward. Dr. Hyde suggested bleeding to relieve arterial pressure. This was the approved remedy, and Dr. Twyman agreed. The man was Dr. Twyman's patient, but, as the younger and more forceful of the two physicians, Dr. Hyde more or less took charge. He opened a vein on Colonel Hunton's arm, and drained a pint of blood.

Dr. Twyman suggested that this was enough. Dr. Hyde thought not, and drained another pint. Dr. Twyman sought to be tactful, and told a story which ended with "The remedy is sometimes worse than the disease." Dr. Hyde pointed out that Colonel Hunton's face was still flushed, and Dr. Twyman replied that Colonel Hunton was always florid. Dr. Hyde continued to bleed the patient, and Dr. Twyman became very agitated. He tipped up the bucket and said sharply: "That's enough blood to take from any man." Mrs. Hyde was holding Colonel Hunton's head, and said: "Dear, don't you think you had better stop? Dr. Twyman wants you to stop." Dr. Hyde then did stop. Colonel Swope's nurse, who had come downstairs to help care for Colonel Hunton, measured the blood taken as six full cups, given afterward as equal to two quarts. Colonel Hunton gasped and died while his arm was being bandaged.

Dr. Twyman was abrupt, and said nothing more about the bleeding. He thought of the episode only as a difference of opinion. Colonel Hunton had certainly had a stroke; Dr. Twyman always thought he would have died with or without bleeding. Dr. Hyde was suspected of nothing, even though immediately after Colonel Hunton's death he gave evidence of his financial interest in the matter. He spoke to Colonel Swope's nurse, saying he wanted to see her alone. As soon as she could, she went to the sitting room upstairs. "Isn't this awful," Dr. Hyde began, and mentioned that Colonel Hunton had been named as an executor in Colonel Swope's will. "I want you to do me a favor," he continued. "Now that Hunton is gone the old man will make a new will in a few days and I want you to get me appointed an executor in Hunton's place, because Colonel Swope has in mind a man named

Hawthorne, a justice of the peace. I'm not a businessman, but I can be. You have influence with the old man; you can easily do this for me."

The nurse said she was in the house professionally, and could not enter private affairs. Dr. Hyde did not accept her refusal until the following day, when he asked if she had spoken to Colonel Swope about the matter. She replied that she had not and would not. They then discussed Colonel Swope's condition. The nurse said he had spent a good night, and that all that seemed to be bothering him was a little trouble with his digestion. "Isn't there some simple remedy that you could bring to help his digestion?" asked the nurse. "Why yes," replied Dr. Hyde, "I'll bring him a digestive capsule the next time I come." So it was the nurse, as she later testified, who first indirectly suggested the capsule which preceded Colonel Swope's death.

Dr. Hyde took no pains to hide his suspicious actions. He could have bought cyanide in bulk, and himself put it in capsules. Instead he had it put up at the drugstore and charged to his account. He had reminded the nurse of his financial interest in the Swope estate. The next morning at the breakfast table, with four or five members of the family present, he called attention to the fact that he was about to give a capsule to Colonel Swope. He asked the nurse whether the colonel had had his breakfast. She replied that he had. "I've been meaning to give him that digestive capsule before breakfast, but I guess we'd better give it to him anyway," said Dr. Hyde. He and the nurse then went upstairs. Colonel Swope, who always believed in testing the strength of a request with two or three refusals, said that he would not take the medicine. The nurse suggested that Dr. Hyde leave the capsule, intimating that the patient would take it before long.

This was the second morning after Moss Hunton's death, an event which had deeply grieved Colonel Swope. At his bedside were the Kansas City and Independence papers for the previous day. After Dr. Hyde left, he asked the nurse to find what would interest him in the Kansas City papers. He then took the capsule, and began rereading the Independence account of Colonel Hunton's death. "Poor old Moss, poor old Moss," he kept saying and shaking his head.

Within twenty minutes after taking the capsule, he had a seizure from which he never recovered. The nurse looked up from her papers to see her patient rigid and staring. She called Dr. Hyde. "It's another case like Mr. Hunton's; it's apoplexy," said Dr. Hyde.

The colonel's symptoms, however, were quite different from Hunton's; and Dr. Hyde in this case did not bleed the patient. Colonel Swope's teeth were clenched; his face was bluish and his eyes were wide and set, with the pupils dilated. His hands were clenched into fists, and his arms were drawn up; his legs were rigid, with the knees somewhat raised. From his mouth came a peculiar blowing sound, alternating with a humming sound. After eight or ten minutes of the seizure he regained consciousness momentarily and said: "My God, I feel terrible; I wish I were dead; I wish I hadn't taken that damned medicine." Then he lapsed back into unconsciousness, and remained so for hours. His pulse, at first slow, went to one hundred and forty beats per minute. Dr. Hyde prescribed three injections of a sixtieth of a grain of strychnine, and the nurse gave him these at fifteen-minute intervals. "I would hate to take the consequences if he recovers," commented the nurse. Dr. Hyde asked why. "Don't you remember? He connected his illness with that medicine you gave him."

Colonel Swope died at seven o'clock that night, having

been unconscious ten hours. The cause was given as apoplexy. The *Star* called it a "remarkable coincidence" that Colonel Swope and Colonel Hunton both had died of the same cause within three days; but no implication of foul play was intended. Colonel Swope was very old; his death was sudden without being surprising; his casket was ordered while he was still breathing, and his will which, it was found, was in a pocket of his coat, was read fifteen minutes after he breathed his last. So far, matters had gone well financially for Dr. Hyde. Colonel Swope had died without effecting his charitable intentions, and Mrs. Hyde would inherit $150,000 or so from the residuary of his estate. In addition, $60,000 which Colonel Swope had bequeathed to Colonel Hunton would revert to the general estate.

Soon after Colonel Swope died, a slight change was made in the drinking water arrangements at the Swopes'. Up to this time all the drinking water had been taken from a cistern back of the house. The water was brought to a butler's pantry, and poured into an ice cooler, which consisted of a barrel with a spigot. Sometime during the spring or summer of 1909, Dr. Hyde had mentioned to Mrs. Swope that the cistern was not the best source for water, that distilled water from the drugstore would be better. He pointed out that there was an open privy in the back yard, and said that unless something was done there might be typhoid fever in the family. Not much attention had been paid to this recommendation, and the Hydes had continued to drink the cistern water, as did all members of the Swope household.

However, a few days after Colonel Swope's death, a five-gallon bottle of distilled water was brought to the house. From it, a smaller bottle was filled and placed in the refrigerator downstairs. Mrs. Hyde, later when defending her husband, said that she had had the distilled water delivered and took much of the responsibility. As others in the family remembered, it was brought by Dr. Hyde. In any case, after early October the Hydes were drinking water from bottles kept in the refrigerator, while the Swopes continued to drink cistern water from the cooler in the butler's pantry.

At about the same time, Dr. Hyde telephoned his friend, Dr. Edward L. Stewart, and invited him to lunch. Dr. Stewart was a pathologist and bacteriologist, and did Dr. Hyde's laboratory work. There was some general talk, during the course of which Dr. Stewart offered to place Dr. Hyde's name in nomination for the presidency of the Jackson County Medical Association. Dr. Hyde "seemed pleased." Then the conversation drifted to Dr. Stewart's specialty. Dr. Hyde said he had often thought he would like to do a little work in bacteria. He said he didn't expect to become a bacteriologist, but that he was interested in the subject and would like to study it a bit. He asked if Dr. Stewart would help him. Dr. Stewart said he would. They discussed the laboratory equipment that would be necessary, and there the matter rested for the time being.

On November 10, Mrs. Hyde had some sharp words with her mother. Mrs. Swope wished the members of the family to sign their shares of the $60,000 in Hunton money over to Hunton's surviving sister. Mrs. Hyde refused. "This is Clark Hyde's work," said Mrs. Swope. "He doesn't love you at all; he only wants your money; he can't bear to see you." The daughter remembered that Mrs. Swope added: "I'll see that he doesn't get any of the Swope money"; but the mother did not recall making this threat. On this and other occasions, it appeared that, whatever had occurred in the past, the principal thing Mrs. Swope had against Dr. Hyde was that he did not love her daughter. In spite of the sharp words, the quarrel did not seem serious. Mrs. Hyde said she had not even spoken to Dr. Hyde concerning the Hunton money.

The following day, November 11, Dr. Hyde bought two dozen culture media at Brecklein's Drug Store. He took six of these to Dr. Stewart's office to be planted with germs. Dr. Stewart planted one with typhoid, and the others with a variety of bacteria. Dr. Hyde picked them up the next day. The tubes contained a standard substance on which germs would grow, and were small enough so that all six of them could be placed in a glass tumbler. On November 16 and 22, Dr. Hyde bought more culture tubes, making a total of two hundred and sixty-one. He said he was planning to set up a laboratory. The tubes were inexpensive, and the total cost was ten or twelve dollars.

Toward the end of November, Mrs. Swope went to Chicago to visit for a week or ten days. On December 2, four members of the Swope family complained that they were not feeling well. On December 3, Dr. Hyde called Dr. Twyman about the illness at the Swope home, and suggested the possibility of typhoid fever. Dr. Twyman said he had no thought of such a thing, that there was no typhoid in town and besides it was too early to tell whether typhoid was present. Dr. Hyde nevertheless seemed convinced that matters would prove serious, and said he would have nurses brought to the house. In Mrs. Swope's absence, Mrs. Hyde would be in charge of the house, he said; but he wanted it understood that Dr. Twyman was to be the physician and "do the doping." Dr. Hyde said he would simply see that Dr. Twyman's instructions were carried out.

The illness proved to be typhoid, and every member of the Swope family then at home contracted the fever. The Hydes, who were drinking water from bottles, were not affected. The colored cook, who drank water from the cistern but kept it in a bucket downstairs, also escaped illness. But the colored housegirl, who drank from the cooler in the butler's pantry, came down with typhoid. Chrisman, Margaret, Stella, and Sarah Swope fell ill; a relative, a former governess, and the seamstress were stricken; a girl who visited one of the Swope daughters overnight contracted the fever—there were ten cases in all.

On December 4, Dr. Hyde telephoned Brecklein's Drug Store and ordered six more five-grain capsules of potassium of cyanide. This time the clerk reported his request to the owner of the drugstore, Hugo Brecklein. Brecklein told the clerk to call back and verify the order, and to have Dr. Hyde call for the poison in person. When Dr. Hyde came to the store, Brecklein reminded him of how dangerous it was to have such a poison in the house, especially in capsules, since they might be mistaken for medicine. Dr. Hyde replied that he wanted to kill some dogs, that he was aware of the danger but that the dogs had annoyed him very much. He promised to let no one else handle the capsules, and to destroy those he did not use; so Brecklein let him have them.

Possibly because poisoning dogs is not a popular pursuit, Dr. Hyde later testified that he said "bugs," meaning cockroaches in his office. However, that could scarcely have made any sense to Brecklein at the time, since the druggist's principal objection was that the poison was in capsules, the least likely form for its use against "bugs." Also, Dr. Hyde's nineteen-year-old office girl testified that, although they had a few roaches in their office, she did not know that they had ever done anything about them. What the prosecution at Hyde's trial noted and stressed was that Dr. Hyde's second purchase of cyanide preceded by only two days the death of Chrisman Swope, Mrs. Swope's thirty-year-old son, who was one of the first to come down with typhoid.

Chrisman Swope was feeling ill on December 2, but kept insisting that he didn't need a doctor. He doped himself profusely with the medicines of Dr. Chasing Hatred Chase Jordan, a Negro of Kansas City, Kansas, who labeled his product "Espanola Herb Medicine" and claimed he was a South American, although he actually hailed from no farther away than Fort Scott, Kansas. He pronounced it "yarb" medicine, and was known to the Swopes as the "Yarb Doctor." Much was made of the use of Dr. Chasing Hatred's medicines in the defense of Dr. Hyde, with the suggestion that these might have been the source of the trouble. But since all of the Swopes had been using the "yarb" medicines off and on for eight years, with no ill effects and possibly some good, it did not appear that they could suddenly have become lethal.

These medicines were used at the Swopes with no great conviction as to their merit. Before Chrisman Swope consented to admit that he was really sick, he sent his sister, Mrs. Hyde, for one of the "yarb" potions. She was unable to find exactly what he wanted, and remarked to another sister that she was taking him some aspirin and he would never know the difference. The possibility of typhoid had been recognized at that time, but it had not occurred to anyone that the attacks would prove especially serious. All of the patients were insisting that they would soon be all right.

Dr. Twyman saw Chrisman Swope on Sunday morning, December 5. A test showed he had typhoid. His temperature was 101, and his pulse was in the eighties. He said he felt perfectly well, as though he were not sick at all. However,

William Rockhill Nelson

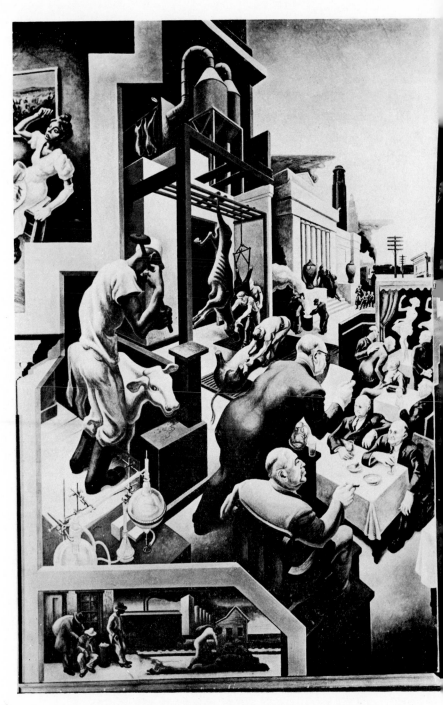

Kansas City panel in the mural painted for the
State Capitol by Thomas Hart Benton

by 2:45 P.M. that day his temperature had risen to 103⅖ and his pulse was ninety-six. Although not alarming, his condition from typhoid had grown steadily worse before he, too, received a capsule from the hand of Dr. Hyde. At 3:00 P.M. his nurse—five nurses had been brought to the house—came into the room and found Dr. Hyde with the patient. It was then time to give Chrisman a fever capsule. Dr. Hyde said he had already given this to him, and left the room.

About twenty minutes later, Chrisman had a seizure, very like Colonel Swope's. The first phase lasted for fifteen minutes. Like Colonel Swope, he regained consciousness momentarily, long enough to say, "Don't worry, mother, we will be all right," and then lapsed into a rigid coma. Dr. Hyde was found and called back. "What happened to Chrisman?" he asked. "It looks like meningitis," said the nurse. Dr. Hyde looked over the patient and concluded: "That's what it is." Colonel Hunton's and Colonel Swope's symptoms had been altogether different, but he had found both those deaths due to apoplexy. Colonel Swope's and Chrisman Swope's symptoms were very similar, but now he found meningitis.

Dr. Twyman was also called and arrived with his son, the younger Dr. Twyman. The three doctors stood over Chrisman. The younger Dr. Twyman held a lighted match in front of Chrisman's set, dilated eyes, and they did not contract. The elder Dr. Twyman raised his legs, and the knees did not bend. It required considerable force to pull one of his arms out straight. His face was bluish, and his pulse so rapid that Dr. Twyman could not count it with any degree of accuracy. Dr. Hyde called it cerebral spinal meningitis. The younger Dr. Twyman said if it was it wasn't the usual kind. The elder Dr. Twyman didn't say anything.

At 2:45 P.M., before taking the capsule, Chrisman's respiration had been thirty-two. At 6:00 P.M. it was only eleven, indicating that he might be suffering from a respiratory poison, possibly cyanide of potassium. He remained in the coma through the night. The next morning his fever rose fearfully, at one time going above 107. He had symptoms of possible poisoning, possible meningitis and, certainly, a severe case of typhoid. But he was a young man, and his resistance was strong.

Toward noon of December 6, he roused in a frenzy. It required the combined strength of the younger Dr. Twyman and the nurse to keep him in bed. He was having hallucinations, imagining that his sister Margaret was dead and that Dr. Hyde was going to operate on him for appendicitis. "Doc, Dr. Hyde is going to operate on me; he's deceiving me," he said. In the afternoon Chrisman showed signs of recovery. His pulse slowed, and he talked rationally. He remembered that he had been struggling, and said: "Say, it must have taken eight men to hold me." The house of many patients, which had been steeled for the loss of a son, picked up hope. When Dr. Hyde arrived a little after four o'clock, Mrs. Swope said: "Doctor, Chrisman is so much better that I believe he is going to get well." "Isn't that fine," said Dr. Hyde, taking off his coat and hurrying to Chrisman's room. The nurse said Chrisman had recovered from his frenzy, but was very weak. Dr. Hyde looked over the patient and said: "He is getting along fine. It is time to begin with his medicine again."

Another capsule from the hand of Dr. Hyde—given to the nurse, who gave it to the patient—was followed by another seizure. This was unlike the first; there was no shock; he grew active, and again doctor and nurse struggled with patient. Then Dr. Hyde told the nurse to go to dinner, and he would stay with the patient. When she came back Chrisman was lying across the bed, and the family was gathered around him. He never revived, and died in an hour and a half. Dr. Twyman shook his head and remarked to his son that he wasn't satisfied with the meningitis theory. He said the picture wasn't clear to him. But he didn't know what else it could be. The son didn't know either. There was still no suspicion of Dr. Hyde.

The night following Chrisman Swope's death, Dr. Hyde was elected president of the Jackson County Medical Association. On December 9, he called Brecklein's Drug Store and ordered twelve more five-grain capsules of cyanide. On December 10, he handed a capsule to Stella Swope and said: "Stella, will you please give this to Miss Gordon (a nurse) to be given to Sarah if she is restless tonight?" What the result of that might have been was not determined, because Sarah Swope, fourteen years old, was not restless during the night, and the nurse threw away the capsule.

At Dr. Hyde's suggestion, three doctors were brought to the Swopes to search for the source of the typhoid. They found nothing definite. Two of the doctors thought the typhoid might have survived from an illness which had afflicted the cook's ten-year-old daughter the previous January. The child's malady had not been satisfactorily diagnosed, but it was thought that she had had typhoid. The third doctor said he couldn't think of there being a "permanent source" of the typhoid, and remarked that everything in the case seemed to "resemble more the operation of a scientific experiment." He suggested that the typhoid must have been brought into the house in "one lump," on bread or other food. Dr. Hyde merely asked whether it could have been brought in on lettuce.

Nowhere did Dr. Hyde give evidence of being a man with anything to fear. He gave a smoker at one of the hotels, to celebrate his election to the presidency of the medical association, and seemed to enjoy himself. Likewise at the Swopes he appeared to be in a good humor. If the typhoid had proved fatal to each of the Swopes who contracted it, he would have benefited to the extent of a million dollars or more through his wife's inheritance; or, if the entire family could have been made to disappear, he would have stepped into the entire Swope fortune. But in the course of things, a number of persons had become ill who had nothing to do with the Swope estate. One of these was Nora Belle Dickson, a former governess who was visiting the Swopes. Miss Dickson afterward recalled a light remark of Dr. Hyde's which she had thought at the time was some kind of joke. After looking at her chart and tapping it meditatively, he had asked: "Miss Dickson, how would you like to take an empty capsule?" Miss Dickson didn't reply; she dismissed it as a remark which she hadn't understood.

The word "poison" was first used in the Swope household on Sunday, December 12. Two or three days before, Dr. Hyde had given some headache powders to Mrs. Swope, who had suffered from headaches for twenty years. "Here are some headache powders I would like you to try," he had said, tossing them on the table. On Sunday he asked if she had taken them. Finding that she had not, he suggested she take one then, and looked around for a capsule to contain one of the powders. For once he couldn't find a capsule. He brought her one of the powders on a piece of paper, poured it on her tongue and handed her a glass of water. She took a few swallows of the water, and it tasted bitter. "Where in the world did you get this water? What are you trying to do, poison me?" she said. She demanded an emetic. Dr. Hyde said he didn't have an emetic, but could give her an injection of appimorphia. "No, you won't give me an injection of anything; you get me an emetic!" Mrs. Swope, a woman of the strongest will, was somewhat aroused at this point, and Dr. Hyde actually did go to the housekeeper and get her a teaspoonful of something. She vomited twice in five minutes, and suffered nothing worse than the headache with which she started. During the incident, Mrs. Hyde said: "Why mother, Clark wouldn't give you poison."

However, these were both innocent uses of the word "poison," such as might occur in any household. As Mrs. Swope later described her thoughts, she had something weighing heavily on her mind at that time, but she didn't know what it was. Certainly she had not allowed herself to think that her son was poisoned. There had been only one occasion when, as it seemed later, she had hinted suspicion. One evening when Dr. Twyman was there, she had said: "Dr. Twyman, is Dr. Hyde all right?" "Yes, Mrs. Swope, I think he is," said Dr. Twyman. That was all; she didn't explain why she asked, and didn't know why she asked, and he didn't inquire. The question had floated in out of nowhere, and the subject was dropped.

CHAPTER FIFTEEN

Suspicion of Hyde

DR. EDWARD L. STEWART, the bacteriologist who had provided Dr. Hyde with the typhoid germs for study, was the first to become really suspicious. On December 13, Dr. Stewart talked to a physician who mentioned the strangeness of the "epidemic" at the Swopes, when there was no typhoid anywhere else. Dr. Stewart thought of how easy it would have been for Dr. Hyde to start the epidemic by dropping the germs into drinking water, and became disturbed about his own possible involvement. He decided to give information to the authorities if necessary. But he had no proof that anything out of the way had occurred, and he did not want to risk damaging Dr. Hyde's reputation with an unjustifiable accusation.

The next day he went to Dr. Hyde's office, with the idea of trying to determine the facts. Dr. Hyde had gone to New York with two other relatives to meet another of the many Swope daughters, Lucy Lee, who was in Europe at the time of Chrisman's death and was cabled to return. Dr. Stewart told Dr. Hyde's office girl that he had come to get Dr. Hyde's typhoid culture, because his own had died. He found the culture in a glass on a shelf, and the girl let him take it.

Upon examining the culture, Dr. Stewart found that enough typhoid germs had been scraped off to inoculate the whole of Kansas City. Still, he had no proof that the germs had been used for other than legitimate purposes, such as an experiment, or possibly making a vaccine. In order to hold the evidence, and still not make his suspicions known, he decided to keep Dr. Hyde's typhoid culture, and return in place of it a tube of non-virile typhoid germs. He planted a second tube with typhoid bacteria, killed the bacteria with formaldehyde fumes, and scraped the dead germs off the upper half of the media so that it would appear the same as the culture he had taken. He returned this harmless tube to Dr. Hyde's office.

Dr. Hyde returned from New York on December 17. On December 18, he entered the sick room of twenty-one-year-old Margaret Swope, shortly after eight o'clock in the morning. He examined the medicines on her dresser. Margaret and the nurse were sure he had picked up the box of capsules she was taking. He asked the nurse when Margaret would next take her medicine. The nurse said eight-thirty, and he left just before that time. Margaret then took a capsule, and within twenty minutes had a seizure which was very like those of Colonel Swope and Chrisman Swope. But unlike them, when Margaret momentarily regained consciousness she was vomiting profusely. Instead of falling back into a rigid coma, she fell into a very deep sleep.

Margaret recovered, but her seizure was the last straw with the nurses. The nurses had had some earlier suspicions, which had not exactly formed as such. For instance, if things seemed to be going well in the house, one of the nurses would say: "Wait till Dr. Hyde gets here; something will be sure to happen." But after Margaret's seizure, the five nurses gave voice to their suspicions, and found they had been sharing similar thoughts. They decided to act together, and delivered an ultimatum to Dr. Twyman: Either Dr. Hyde must be barred from the house or they, the nurses, would leave in a body.

Dr. Twyman at first admitted that the happenings were mysterious. After some thought, however, he returned to protest that he could not imagine anyone so low in the scale of humanity as even to conceive of such an enormous crime. He said he was certain the nurses must be mistaken. One of the nurses suggested that perhaps Dr. Twyman's life had not been the same as Dr. Hyde's, and that sometimes the truth was difficult to imagine. "Now Dr. Twyman," said the nurse, "you can talk all you please, you are not going to convince us at all, because we think we know that Dr. Hyde is responsible for the death of Colonel Swope and Chrisman Swope, and the inoculation of this family with typhoid."

At Dr. Twyman's request, the nurses agreed to stay one more day. He told Mrs. Swope of the nurses' suspicions. She said, "Oh God, do they think that? Then it must be true." It came to her then that the same suspicion had been weighing on her own mind. Finally, Dr. Twyman himself began to think that something had been terribly wrong. He left word for Dr. Hyde to telephone him that evening. He talked to the Swope family attorney. When Dr. Hyde called, Dr. Twyman knew what he wanted to say. He asked Dr. Hyde to come to his office. Dr. Hyde asked if Dr. Twyman couldn't come to the house. Dr. Twyman said the matter was "very delicate," and that he would prefer to talk to him alone.

So when Dr. Hyde left the Swopes a little before 8:30 P.M.

on December 18, he knew that Dr. Twyman wished to speak of something "very delicate." He may not have been too certain that Dr. Twyman would be alone. It was medium dark; the street lights were lit, and there was snow on the ground. Dr. Hyde proceeded north toward Dr. Twyman's office, walking on the east side of Pleasant Street. Young Thomas H. Swope, a married son, had taken his sister, Lucy Lee, to a neighbor's to stay for the night, and was returning to the Swopes. He was walking south on the west side of Pleasant Street. From a distance of about a block and a half, Swope saw a man coming north on the other side of the street. Then he saw him, in two different places, drop something into the snow and stamp on it vigorously with his foot. Finally, the man came under a street light, and Swope recognized Dr. Hyde.

Swope continued south, then crossed the street and doubled back to see what Dr. Hyde had stamped into the snow. He struck a match over one of the places, and saw some pieces of capsules. He picked up the largest piece he saw, and carried it to the Swope home in his hand. He found there was a strong odor clinging to his hand, one which he couldn't wash off and which remained for twenty-four hours. Around this circumstance developed an odd feature of the case. Tom Swope had worked in a stamp mill where gold ores were tested, and therefore was familiar with cyanide. One of the nurses had worked in a jeweler's shop and had used cyanide to clean jewelry. Yet at the time, neither recognized the odor as being that of cyanide, although they agreed it was like burned almonds— the characteristic smell of cyanide. Both later were sure that the odor was that of cyanide, but their testimony was weakened by the fact that they did not recognize it at the time when there had been no mention of this poison.

When Dr. Hyde reached the office, Dr. Twyman came

directly to the point. "Dr. Hyde," he said, "the matter I have to talk to you about is delicate and I am loath to do so, but I don't know any way to get around it. I have studied the matter over and from the standpoint of duty there is nothing to do but tell you that the nurses are up in arms and are going to leave unless you do. They have the idea that you are responsible for all the trouble there; they refuse to stay any longer if you stay in the house."

"Well, that's pretty bad, isn't it?" said Dr. Hyde. "Tell me some more; talk some more about it, tell me what they say."

Dr. Twyman was a good deal more ill at ease than was Dr. Hyde, and he continued in a formal way: "Dr. Hyde, if you wish it, I will tell you what they say. They say that Colonel Swope was in his ordinary state of health and that you prescribed a capsule which he first refused to take and finally took under pressure and had a convulsion twenty or thirty minutes afterwards, dying in about eight hours, and they believe you killed him. In the next place, Chrisman Swope Sunday morning had a temperature of 101 and a pulse of eighty and was feeling fine, and between three and four o'clock he had a convulsion and the nurses think you doped him. The nurses think you have inoculated this family with typhoid germs—brought the typhoid culture there and fed it to them. They believe you are trying to kill the family for their money."

"Well, that looks pretty bad; that is a terrible accusation. I could sue those nurses for a criminal accusation like that."

"What would you gain if you did sue the nurses? If the nurses leave and you make this thing public, people are aware that you married under strong protest; and I want to say to you, doctor, that if this matter is made public there are thousands of people in Kansas City and Jackson County who are going to believe you guilty."

Dr. Hyde agreed that what Dr. Twyman said was true, and commented that there was "no way of meeting a scandal." He was inclined to blame Mrs. Swope for the suspicions against him. He told of the incident in which she had exclaimed "What are you trying to do, poison me?" and said: "I guess that shows what *she* thinks." Then he talked on and on in a rambling conversation. Speaking of scandals, he told of a young woman patient who when she came to him was suing a wealthy man for damages, an action which Dr. Hyde described as blackmail. He had found evidence, he said, that the woman had gone wrong before, and had reported this to the wealthy man. They had succeeded in getting a "confession" from her, and stopping her legal action. Dr. Hyde's betrayal of the patient was against all the tenets of medical practice with which Dr. Twyman was familar; and yet the unmistakable fact was that Dr. Hyde was seeking favor, and expected credit for his act. As he left the office at the conclusion of the interview, Dr. Hyde expressed his good will toward Dr. Twyman, and congratulated him for having done "the manly thing."

Upon his return to the Swopes, Dr. Hyde packed his things and left the house for the last time. Mrs. Swope begged Mrs. Hyde to stay, but she went with her husband. Even after all the suspicions had been aroused, Mrs. Swope mentioned what seems always to have been her principal objection to Dr. Hyde. "He doesn't love her; I'm sure of that," she said. "There's an influence, a hypnotic, overpowering something that will fade some day. Then I think she'll come back to me."

A day or two after Dr. Hyde left the Swopes, Dr. Stewart called at his office. Dr. Stewart asked casually whether he had yet made any use of the typhoid bacilli. Dr. Hyde replied with equal casualness that he had "fooled around a bit." However, Dr. Hyde must have detected a note of suspicion in Dr. Stewart's voice. He must have examined his typhoid culture, and must have discovered that in place of the live germs, he now had a culture of dead germs. For Dr. Hyde accosted his office girl, saying: "Dr. Stewart was in my office for something, wasn't he?" The girl said yes, she had forgotten to mention it, and described Dr. Stewart's borrowing the culture. "You shouldn't have let him; Dr. Stewart may just have been taking advantage of my absence," said Dr. Hyde.

Dr. Hyde, then, knew of Dr. Stewart's suspicions; he knew of the nurses' suspicions; and he knew of his own purchases of cyanide at Brecklein's Drug Store. For a brief period of time, he was probably the only person who knew of more than one of these three key aspects of the case; and he no doubt suspected they would soon be joined. For that reason, although his connection, if any, was never proved, it was always suspected that Dr. Hyde might have had something to do with a fire which on the night of December 22–23 broke out in Brecklein's Drug Store. If so, the fire failed of its purpose. The drugstore was badly gutted, but its poison and account books were undamaged.

Two more cases of typhoid came from the one-family epidemic. One was Lucy Lee Swope, who had been in Europe; and the other was Dr. Hyde himself. Lucy Lee had been cabled to return on December 6 and had been met in New York by the three relatives including Dr. Hyde. The first night on the train, when she started to get a drink of water, Dr. Hyde said: "Wait a minute; I have a folding cup for you."

He produced the cup and obtained the water for her. It tasted all right, and she drank it all. That was on December 15. On December 21 she was feeling ill, and on December 22 she was definitely sick. She had typhoid, but she recovered.

Dr. Hyde's illness was slight, and Dr. Stewart for a time was puzzled by it. Dr. Stewart was called to the Hydes on December 29 to examine Dr. Hyde for typhoid. He made a test and got a positive reaction; there seemed no doubt that Dr. Hyde was suffering from the disease but his symptoms were very mild. Dr. Stewart wondered why Dr. Hyde had also called in two other doctors to examine him for the same illness, and why he was so detailed in listing among his symptoms almost everything that could occur in a severe typhoid case. It seemed to Dr. Stewart that Dr. Hyde was overly anxious to have people think that he was suffering from typhoid, and that he had contracted it at the Swopes.

Dr. Stewart decided to make another test. He took 2½ cubic centimeters of Dr. Hyde's blood, and placed it in 250 cubic centimeters of beef tea—the most fertile soil for the growth of typhoid germs. If there were such germs in Dr. Hyde's blood, they should have multiplied rapidly in this solution. But they didn't; this time Dr. Stewart got a negative result. He concluded that Dr. Hyde had injected himself with dead typhoid germs, which would give him mild symptoms and a positive test (Widal), without the risk of the disease.

Meanwhile the family attorney had been active and Colonel Swope's body was exhumed. Dr. Hyde had been specific in describing the cause of the colonel's death as a cerebral hemorrhage, and as "apoplexy resulting from the rupture of a blood vessel on the left side of his brain." On January 12, 1910, with experts from Chicago and a number of local doctors present, an autopsy was conducted on Colonel

Swope's body, and the brain was found to be in normal condition. There was much wrangling and confusion over the expert testimony given later at the trial, but it seemed scarcely possible that there could have been any mistake on this one point: whatever was the cause, Colonel Swope did not die of a cerebral hemorrhage, as was stated on his death certificate, which was signed by Dr. Hyde.

Open suspicion caught up with Dr. Hyde a few days after he recovered from his brief illness. The first word to reach the public was "flashed" accidentally by a *Star* correspondent in Independence. As the official county seat, Independence furnished a large daily run of small, routine news items. That day a case of chicken thievery had been reported to the authorities. There were visitors at prominent homes, a few marriages, real-estate transfers and the like. Having dictated these items over the telephone, the Independence correspondent considered his day's work done. He lapsed into a friendly conversation, during the course of which he remarked: "You know, a funny thing, they've dug up old Colonel Swope's body."

A *Star* rewrite man quickly got in touch with another of the paper's news sources in Independence. Yes, Colonel Swope's body had been taken from the vault, said the informant, adding that he had known about the matter for several days. "They think he was murdered," said the man in Independence. The rewrite man was in a great hurry, but he allowed himself one anguished question: "*Why* didn't you tell us, so we could put it in our newspaper?" The informant was shocked: "You're not going to *print* that! Why, the Swopes are one of the most prominent families out here."

The *Star* did print it, and one day a little later filled six solid pages with the full details. The first accounts were reticent in involving Dr. Hyde, who was quoted as saying he thought the typhoid at the Swopes came from milk. "I was down with it myself," said Dr. Hyde. "It was a light attack; Dr. Perkins tested my blood and found the germ." But eventually Dr. Hyde was indicted and placed in jail, and the big trial was set. Although a mountain of evidence had accumulated against him, this did not mean that Dr. Hyde was automatically considered guilty. On the contrary, many thought him innocent. They felt the same difficulty Dr. Twyman had experienced, that of imagining a man who could conceive of such an enormous crime. Then, too, there was at the time a strong prejudice against circumstantial evidence, as a number of persons had thus been wrongly convicted. And all of the evidence against Dr. Hyde was circumstantial.

James A. Reed was engaged by the Swopes as special prosecutor, and Frank P. Walsh represented Dr. Hyde. Both of the attorneys were near the age of forty. Both were drawing $50,000 fees. As far as criminal court procedure was concerned, the Hyde trial was the climax of their careers. One of the first events of the trial was the disappearance of the grand jury testimony, from a cubbyhole in the district attorney's office. The next event was the reappearance of the grand jury transcript in the hands of the defense. Walsh said it had been dropped on a sidewalk and turned over to him. There lingers in Kansas City today a suspicion that the fact that Reed was politically a Goat, and Walsh politically a Rabbit, plus the fact that there were two or three Rabbits in the district attorney's office, had a great deal to do with the disappearance and reappearance of the grand jury transcript. Since the grand jury testimony was known both to the prosecution and the defense, it was also published in the newspapers. By the time Dr. Hyde's trial was well under way, almost everything to which a local witness could testify had already been in the papers. Attention was centered on a battery of experts from Chicago, and on what they would say about the poison found in the bodies of Colonel Swope and Chrisman Swope.

These experts, as far as establishing the prosecution's case was concerned, fell down in a number of ways. Two of them, unfortunately, had co-authored a textbook on the subject of autopsies. Walsh held a copy of the textbook in his hand during their cross-examination, and from time to time read passages from it. The book sternly admonished embryonic toxicologists against attempting to remove organs when a body was frozen. "The frozen brain cannot be removed without fatal damage," said the book. Yet this was exactly the condition in which Colonel Swope's brain had been removed. The expert could only say lamely that he was "in a hurry to get to work," and that he had changed his opinions since writing the book. In a number of other instances, Walsh made it appear that the experts did not know what they were doing.

The textbooks definitely said that tests for potassium of cyanide must be made immediately after death. Cyanide coming in contact with moisture, said the books, would become volatile and escape in the form of a gas. Yet these experts claimed to have found traces of cyanide after three or four months; also their tests showed only traces of cyanide—not enough to have caused death. The defense produced expert testimony that a little cyanide might form from a combination of embalming fluid with elements in the body. The only large amount of poison found was the strychnine in Colonel Swope's body. And as was well known, Colonel Swope had been in the habit of dosing himself for dyspepsia